ND THEIR CHARACTERISTICS

(5) Debatable	(6) Vote Required	(7) Refer to Rule	NOTES
		170	
No	Majority	170	(a) As to time and place only; not as to date.
No	Majority	173	
No	Majority	173	
(a)	Majority	174	
(a)	Majority	175	(b) This is a demand or request, not a true motion.
		112	
No	No Vote	83	
No	No Vote	92	
No	No Vote	93	(c) Before it has been stated by the chair it does not require seconding or a vote.
No	No Vote	94	
No	No Vote	95	
No	Majority	128	
No	(g)	147	
		111	
No	Majority	148	(d) Debate restricted to wisdom of dividing.
No	Majority	148	
(e)	(g)	144	
(e)	(g)	144	
Yes	(g)	145	
(f)	(g)	146	(e) As to date and time only.
Yes	(g)	133	
Yes (d)	No Vote	120	
Yes (d)	Majority	121	
		110	(f) As to conditions of reference.
Yes	(g)	124	
Yes	(g)	125	
Yes	(h)	110	
No	Unanimous	126	(g) Requires the same majority as does the main motion to which it applies.
		96	
No	—	97	
No	Majority	98	
No	Majority	99	(h) Requires the majority fixed by the statute or the constitution.
No	Majority	101	
No	Majority	102	

COMPANY MEETINGS

including

RULES OF ORDER

COMPANY MEETINGS

including

RULES OF ORDER

By

J. M. WAINBERG, Q.C.

OF THE ONTARIO BAR

THIRD EDITION

C C H Canadian Limited

PUBLISHERS OF TOPICAL LAW REPORTS

HEAD OFFICE: 6 Garamond Ct., Don Mills, Ont. M3C 1Z5. Telephone (416) 441-2992

Commerce House, Suite 728
1080 Beaver Hall Hill
Montreal, Que. H2Z 1S8
(514) 866-2771

130 Albert St.
Ottawa, Ontario
K1P 5G4
(613) 235-8414

1260 Bow Valley Square 3
255 - 5 Ave. S.W.
Calgary, Alberta T2P 3G6
(403) 269-2169

Three Bentall Centre
Suite 2423 - P.O. Box 49216
Vancouver, B.C. V7X 1K8
(604) 688-7510

4124

First Edition 1961

Second Edition 1969

Third Edition 1982
Second Printing, January, 1984
Third Printing, June, 1985

Canadian Cataloguing in Publication Data

Wainberg, J. M., 1906–
  Company meetings including rules of order

Includes index.
ISBN 0-88798-180-0

1. Corporate meetings – Canada. 2. Corporation law –
Canada. I. CCH Canadian Limited. II. Title.

KE1434.W35 1982   346.71'066450269   C82-095211-7

ISBN 0-88796-180-0

PRINTED IN CANADA

PREFACE

In my preface to the first edition I noted that "Company meetings in Canada are conducted according to procedures laid down by precedent and common law emanating from British parliamentary practice. On the whole, statutes are silent as to the conduct of meetings, and bylaws have as many versions as there are lawyers."

For the backbone of the text I had to draw primarily on my own experience in the conduct of meetings and in proxy fights for control of companies, as well as from ensuing litigation.

Again I had the invaluable assistance of my son, Mark Irwin Wainberg, who helped to further my aim to make this work clear and terse with logical arrangement and sequence.

This third edition has been not only updated but completely revised. New rules and new cases have been added. The index has been enlarged to ensure quick reference.

A word of caution: the law relating to conduct of meetings is not the same on all points in Canada as in the U.S.A. or even in England and Australia. Whereas all the acts and rules derive from the Mother of Parliaments, each child has developed differently. Some genes have survived, others have mutated to reflect the times and the people.

Accordingly caution must be exercised in trying to apply U.S. or English rules of order to Canadian situations. They do not all apply.

Another caution: rules for the conduct of meetings of societies, clubs and associations are not always identical to the rules applicable to business corporations. *Wainberg's Society Meetings, Including Rules of Order* (now in preparation) will cover this subject.

J. M. W.

Toronto, September, 1982.

v

TABLE OF CONTENTS

GLOSSARY

Accept

To receive. Acceptance of a report does not necessarily mean endorsement of its recommendations. A factual statement is "accepted", a report is "accepted". However, a recommendation is "adopted". (*See* "Adopt".)

Adopt

To concur. To adopt a report is to concur with its recommendations and agree to implement them in some form. Recommendations and resolutions are "adopted". (*See* "Verify".)

Adjourn

To defer to another day. An adjournment may be "*cum die*"—that is, to a fixed day—or, "*sine die*"—without a fixed day. If all the business for which the meeting was called has been dealt with, the meeting should be "concluded". (*See* "Conclude", "Terminate", "Recess" and "Postpone".)

Adjourned meeting

A continuation of a meeting after an adjournment or recess.

Agenda

A list of things to be done; the order of business to be brought up, discussed and disposed of.

Amend

To change by adding, deleting or substituting words.

Amendment

A motion to vary the motion under discussion.

Announcement

See "Declaration".

Apply

A motion "applies" to another when it alters, affects or disposes of the original motion.

Appointment

The act of naming for an office (Rule 102). No choice is implied. (*See* "Election".)

Approve

To adopt. To ratify. Sometimes incorrectly used when verifying minutes of meetings. (*See* "Verify".) Annual reports are "approved".

Ballot

A paper (either printed or blank) on which the voter records his vote.

Bylaw

(Omitting the hyphen is supported by good authority.) A permanent, continuing rule to be applied to future occasions, in contrast to a resolution, which applies only to a single act of a corporation. (*See* "Special Bylaw".)

Call to order

The act by the chairman at the beginning of a meeting of requesting the attention of those present and assuming his authority.

Casting vote

A second vote by the chairman exercisable in addition to his own vote as a director or shareholder, permissible only if specifically granted by the constitution.

Chair

The chairman or presiding officer. The chairman refers to himself, and is referred to, as the "chair".

Chairman

The presiding officer.

Committee

A group of shareholders or directors to whom a matter is referred for deliberation, study, action, or recommendation (*see Re Taurine Co.* (1883), 25 Ch. D. 118; *Reynell v. Lewis* (1846), 15 M. & W. 517, at p. 529, 153 E.R. 954). A committee may be discharged at any time by the authority appointing it.

Common law

Law based upon court decisions and general custom.

Conclude meeting

To bring to a close after completion of all business. To "terminate meeting" is to close without completing the business of the meeting.

Confirm

Ratify; sanction. Certain bylaws and resolutions must be confirmed by the shareholders before becoming effective. *See* "Verify" for minutes.

Consideration, object to

See "Object to Consideration".

Constitution

The lifeblood of the corporation; the memorandum of association, articles, letters patent and bylaws.

Convene

To formally open a meeting.

Cum die

To a fixed day. (*See* "Adjourn".)

Debate

Discussion; an open argument for or against a motion.

Declaration

A decision of the chairman. (*See* Rule 155.)

De facto directors

Persons not duly elected as directors who act as directors.

Demand

A request made to the chairman for action by him. (*See* table on inside of front cover.)

Election

The act of choosing or selecting one or more from a number of people making a choice by any manifestation of preference. "Appointing" is merely the act of naming for an office. (*See* "Appointment".) *See* Rules 96—101.

Expunge

To delete or obliterate a resolution or comment from the minutes.

Floor

The right to speak. The person who "has the floor" has the right to speak and no one else may speak, except in strict accordance with the rules, until the chairman gives the floor to another. A subject on the floor or on the table is a subject before the meeting.

Germane

Pertaining or relating directly to the subject.

Information, point of

See "Point of information".

Inquiry,

See "Parliamentary Inquiry".

Lay on the table

To lay a matter on the table, or to table a matter, is to open it up for discussion. Caution must be exercised when reading American texts. In the United States to "lay on the table" means to suspend further discussion or to "shelve" (*see* "Shelve"). The English and Canadian meaning is to open for discussion. It would be preferable to use "presented for discussion".

Main motion

A proposal put to the meeting for discussion and decision (*see* "Motion").

Majority

More than half. It may apply to more than half of the shareholders, or to more than half of the voting stock, or to more than half of the votes cast (*see* "Resolution" and "Special Resolution").

Meeting

The coming together of two or more persons with the common intention of transacting business. A session is part of a meeting (*see* "Session").

Minority

Less than half. (*See* "Majority".)

Minutes

The official record of a meeting or a session.

Motion

A proposal to do something, to order something to be done, or to express an opinion about something. The subject matter of the motion is called a "question". A motion when duly passed becomes a resolution.

Nominate

To propose someone to an office to be filled. (Rule 97.)

Object to consideration

A motion to drop the subject. A motion objecting to the consideration of the motion being discussed must be made before it is seconded or while the first speaker on it is discussing it. (Rule 147.)

Out of order

Contrary to parliamentary procedure or *ultra vires*. Irrelevant. Not germane.

Parliamentary inquiry

A request for information on a matter of parliamentary procedure.

Point of information

A question requesting and permitting a factual answer regarding the content or background of a motion. (Rule 94.)

Point of order

A request to correct a situation which violates a rule of parliamentary procedure. (Rule 92.)

Point of (personal) privilege

See "Privilege".

Poll

A common law method of voting by which each voter by his personal act delivers his vote to a chairman, or answers a roll call.

Postpone

To defer a discussion which has not commenced. (*See* "Adjourn".)

Precedence

Designates rank. (*See* "Rank".) Certain motions have precedence over others.

Previous question

A motion to close discussion, terminate debate or vote immediately. (*Archaic term*)

Privilege

The right to immediate consideration (without a seconder) of a matter which affects the meeting or any individual thereof regarding safety, orderliness, comfort or honour.

Privileged motion

A motion having a high priority. A motion to conclude, terminate, or adjourn, has the highest priority.

Procedural motion

A motion dealing with procedure as distinguished from a substantive motion.

Proposition

A suggestion not yet formally phrased as a motion or a resolution. The chairman may sometimes permit a general conversation around a subject with the intent that a resolution or a motion will evolve therefrom.

Proxy

A signed power of attorney authorizing someone (who may or may not be a shareholder, depending on the bylaws) to act on behalf of a shareholder at a meeting. (*See* "Proxyholder".)

Proxy form

An unsigned power of attorney.

Proxyholder

The agent or attorney of a shareholder. (*See* "Proxy".)

Putting the question

Putting the motion to a vote. A motion to vote immediately. (*See* "Previous question".)

Question

The subject matter of a motion or discussion.

Quorum

The minimum number of qualified persons whose presence at a meeting is requisite in order that business may be legally transacted.

Rank

Rank or priority settles the precedence of the motion, or the right of way of one motion over another. A motion to adjourn has a higher rank than any other motion.

Ratify

To confirm or make valid by formal consent in writing. To approve of an act after it has been done, or approve of an agreement after it has been executed.

Recess

A short interruption of a meeting or a session of a meeting. This is shorter than an adjournment. Recess is usually for a matter of minutes or a few hours at most, for the purpose of comfort, lunch, permitting factions to meet to settle a dispute, or to count ballots.

Recognize

The chairman "recognizes" the shareholder thereby giving him the floor and the right to speak. This may be done by calling out the name of a shareholder, or otherwise signalling to him that he may speak. (*See* "Floor".)

Reconsider

To review again the matter previously disposed of. To open up a matter disposed of, to re-discuss for the purpose of voting on it again.

Repeal

See "Rescind".

Rescind

To cancel, quash, void or nullify a resolution.

Resolution

A corporate resolve; the result of a motion that requires only a simple majority that has been passed (*see* "Special resolution").

Rules of order

The rules as enumerated in this text.

Scrutineer

A clerk or teller appointed by the chairman or by the meeting to assist the chairman in counting the attendance, collecting and examining and tabulating proxies and ballots.

Second a motion

To consent to a motion being discussed by the meeting. Seconding does not necessarily approve of the motion itself.

Sense of the meeting

The opinion, decision or feeling of those present; need not be unanimous.

Session

A sitting or part of a meeting. It may be that portion of the meeting which is held before noon, or the portion held in the afternoon, both of which together constitute a meeting.

Shelve

To suspend or put away; suspend any further consideration of a matter.

Show of hands

An informal method of voting which eliminates the necessity for taking a poll, unless a poll is demanded.

Silent assent

Assumption of general concurrence based on the fact that no objection is voiced; acquiescence.

Sine die

Wtihout a date being fixed. (*See* "Adjourn".)

Sitting

See "Session".

Special bylaw

A bylaw requiring confirmation by a majority of two-thirds or more of the shareholders. (*See* "Bylaw".)

Special resolution

A resolution requiring more than a simple majority. (*See* "Resolution".) In Ontario a special resolution is a resolution passed by a two-thirds majority at a special meeting or consented to in writing by all the shareholders.

Stating the question

Before calling for a vote the chairman restates the motion clarifying it at the same time if necessary.

Sub-amendment

An amendment to an amendment.

Substantive motion

A main motion. A motion proposing a concrete matter of business as distinguished from a procedural motion.

Table

See "Lay on the Table".

Terminate meeting

See "Conclude".

Unanimous

With no dissenting vote.

Unanimous shareholder agreement

A written agreement between all the shareholders providing for the exercising of their voting rights. It may also provide for restriction of the powers, duties and liabilities of the directors, settlement of disputes and other matters.

Unfinished business

Any business left over from a previous meeting, either by the adjournment of the previous meeting or by a specific motion to postpone a matter to a subsequent meeting.

Verify

To authenticate as true or correct. Minutes of meetings are "verified". Verification does not imply adoption.

Yield

A motion yields to another if that other has a higher precedence or rank. The speaker having the floor may yield the floor to another shareholder of his own volition, or at the request of the chairman. (*See* "Rank".)

PART I

RULES OF ORDER

INTRODUCTION

The paramount purpose of parliamentary procedure is to democratically ascertain the will of the majority and to see that their will is carried out but with fairness and good faith. When the majority decision has been determined by a vote, that vote becomes the decision of the assembly. It is then the duty of the minority to accept and abide by the decision. This is the unwritten law in a democracy. When a member joins the group he tacitly agrees to be governed by the majority.

This submission to the will of the majority is conditional upon the fairness of the majority and the utilization of democratic principles.

Every member has equal rights: the right to speak freely without interruption, to propose motions and to vote. If he is in the majority, he has the obligation to protect the rights of the minority. If he is in the minority, he has the right to expect the protection of the majority in the presentation of his democratic rights.

Under the rules that have developed over the years through the decisions of the courts, a meeting cannot act contrary to the wishes of the majority. No resolution may be passed, agreement entered into, or money expended without the approval of the majority.

The rights of the minority are protected by the quorum rule, the right to be heard, the right to enter into the discussion on any motion, the right to make a motion and have it considered and the right of the minority, as well as of the absentees, to expect that the governing statute, the constitution and the rules of order will be followed.

British parliamentary procedure is the root of all rules of order for the conduct of meetings of societies, of the public and of governmental bodies throughout the English speaking world. Parliamentary rules have been changed by statute or usage. Some changes are minor, others are of great importance. In Parliament, an appeal from a ruling of the chair may usually be made to the members. In the case of company meetings, some appeals from rulings of the chair may be made to the members, others, only to the courts. At common law, shareholders were once required to appear in person to voice their opinions and cast their votes. Statutes now permit them to appoint agents (proxyholders) to attend meetings and vote on their behalf.

Confusion concerning the meanings of the word "motion" and "resolution" has been eliminated. In this work, "resolution" is treated as a corporate resolve, and there can hardly be a resolve without a decision. A motion is a proposal which initiates a decision (see Glossary).

It is not claimed that all the rules contained in this work have specific statutory authority. It is, however, contended that these rules are based partly upon common law, as varied by statute, and partly upon parliamentary law, as varied by accepted usage. In a few places, where a hiatus appeared to exist, a rule has been enunciated in the spirit of the democratic rights intended to be preserved by parliamentary rules of order.

Although a number of these rules may also apply to societies, associations and other non-share corporations, most do not apply. See *Wainberg's Society Meetings, Including Rules of Order* now in preparation.

CHAPTER I

MEETINGS

MEETINGS GENERALLY

1. Rules of order

Meetings of shareholders and of the board of directors are governed by the same democratic principles which apply to parliamentary bodies. These principles embody fairness, reasonableness, and good faith towards all who are entitled to take part. Rules of order are framed towards this end. Every constitution[1] should provide that all meetings be governed by a specific manual of rules of order. It is the chairman's duty to enforce and the obligation of the shareholders and directors to insist upon the enforcement of the designated rules of order.[2]

2. Coming together

A meeting is the coming together of two or more persons with the common intention of transacting business. To constitute a valid meeting there must be a common intention that the coming together is a meeting of shareholders or of directors.[3]

---

[1] Wherever the word "constitution" appears it means the memorandum of association and articles or the letters patent and bylaws or articles of incorporation and bylaws.

[2] Rule 68.

[3] The word "meeting" implies a concurrence or coming to face of at least two persons: *Sharp v. Dawes* (1876), 2 Q.B.D. 26; *Re Sanitary Carbon Co.*, [1877] W.N. 223.

3. Irregularity

The meeting must be called and held in accordance with the governing statute and the constitution. An inherent irregularity in connection with the calling of the meeting (e.g., not notifying all entitled to be notified,[4] or not giving the required length of notice[5]) invalidates the proceedings thereat.[6]

> *Comment:* Strict compliance with statutory provisions is required. The court will not use its equitable powers to read something into a statute which is not there stated.[7]

4. Acquiescence

Some irregularities may be cured[8] or waived by the acquiescence of those affected,[9] but acquiescence by the shareholders (or the directors) will not enable a company to do an act which is *ultra vires* or illegal.

> *Comment:* Acquiescence could cure the failure to hold a meeting or nonconformity with statutory requirements with respect to voting.[10] Acquiescence, whether expressed or implied, or delay in raising an objection may operate as an estoppel or may be deemed to be ratification.[11]

5. Control of the meeting

The control of the meeting is the responsibility of the chairman.[12] Some questions relating to the conduct of the meeting are

---

4 Rule 48.

5 Rule 40.

6 *McDougall v. Black Lake Asbestos & Chrome Co. Ltd.* (1920), 47 O.L.R. 328; *Canadian Ohio Motor Car Co. v. Cochrane* (1915), 7 O.W.N. 698, aff'd 8 O.W.N. 242; *Kelly v. Electrical Construction Co.* (1907), 16 O.L.R. 232; *Sovereen Mitt, Glove, and Robe Co. v. Whitside* (1906), 12 O.L.R. 638; *Waddell v. Ontario Canning Co.* (1889), 18 O.R. 41; *School Section No. 16 Trustees v. Cameron* (1878), 2 S.C.R. 690. See Rule 4.

7 *McKenna v. Spooner Oils Ltd.,* [1934] 1 W.W.R. 255; *Pacific Coast Coal Mines Ltd. v. Arbuthnot* (1917), 36 D.L.R. 564; *Re Carpenter Ltd.; Hamilton's Case* (1916), 29 D.L.R. 683; *Sherker v. Rudner* (1910), 39 Que. S.C. 44; *Towers v. African Tug Co.,* [1904] 1 Ch. 558; *Colonist Printing and Publishing Co. v. Dunsmuir* (1902), 32 S.C.R. 679.

8 Rules 23, 58, 59.

9 *Classic Hosiery Co. Ltd. v. Fillis* (1920), 18 O.W.N. 17.

10 *Farmers Bank v. Sunstrum* (1909), 14 O.W.R. 288; *Re Scottish Petroleum Co.* (1882), 23 Ch. D. 413; *Re Alma Spinning Co.* (1880), 16 Ch. D. 681.

11 *Patterson v. Vulcan Iron Works Ltd.,* [1929] 4 D.L.R. 508, aff'd [1930] 2 D.L.R. 961; *Re D. & S. Drug Co.* (1916), 31 D.L.R. 643; *Prudential Trust Co. v. Brodeur* (1918), 25 Rev. Leg. (N.S.) 335; *A.-G. (Can.) v. Standard Trust Co. of New York* [1911] A.C. 498; *Adams and Burns v. Bank of Montreal* (1901), 32 S.C.R. 719; *McDougall v. Lindsay Paper Mill Co.* (1884), 10 P.R. 247; *Thompson v. Canada Fire & Marine Ins. Co.* (1884), 6 O.R. 291, rev'd 9 O.R. 284; *Christopher v. Noxon* (1883), 4 O.R. 672.

12 *Carruth v. Imperial Chemical,* [1937] A.C. 707.

under the control of those properly present at the meeting and entitled to vote. They can determine:

— whether notices, resolutions, minutes and financial statements are to be read;

— whether strangers,[13] representatives of the press or other persons not entitled to be present are to be permitted to attend;

— whether scrutineers should be appointed;[14]

— whether and when discussion is to be terminated;[15]

— whether and when the meeting is to be adjourned, and for what period;[16]

— whether and when the meeting is to be concluded;[16]

— whether and to what extent the auditors may be questioned.[16a]

Comment: If necessary the chairman shall take a vote to ascertain the sense of the meeting. The opinion of a majority is sufficient.

6. Majority rule

In the absence of any provision to the contrary in the governing statute[17] and the constitution, all questions are decided by a majority of votes of those present and voting.

A majority vote will bind the minority,[18] provided that the

---

[13] Rule 10.

[14] Rule 78.

[15] Rule 144 etc.

[16] Rule 173 etc.

[16a] Rule 52.

[17] See table inside back cover.

[18] "It is a fundamental principle of corporation law that the will of the majority must prevail." (*Noble v. Cameron*, [1955] 3 D.L.R. 513 at p. 515, following *R. v. Varlo* (1775), 1 Cowp. 248, 98 E.R. 1068.) See also *North-West Transportation Co. Ltd. v. Beatty* (1887), 12 App. Cas. 589; *Edwards v. Halliwell*, [1950] 2 All E.R. 1064; *Re Horbury Bridge Coal, Iron & Waggon Co.* (1879), 11 Ch. D. 109; *Dominion Cotton Mills Co. v. Amyot and Brunet* (1912), 4 D.L.R. 306; *Black v. Carson* (1914), 36 D.L.R. 772; *Garvie v. Axmith* (1961), 31 D.L.R. (2d) 65; *Re Jury Gold Mine Development Co.*, [1928] 4 D.L.R. 735; *Gray v. Yellowknife Gold Mines Ltd. and Bear Exploration & Radium Ltd.*, [1948] 1 D.L.R. 473; *Canada Safeway Ltd. v. Thompson*, [1951] 3 D.L.R. 295; *Canada Safeway Ltd. v. Thompson*, [1952] 2 D.L.R. 591; *Re Leigh; Royal Trust Co. v. Norrie*, [1951] 3 D.L.R. 561; *Gray v. New Augurita Porcupine Mines Ltd.*, [1952] 3 D.L.R. 1; *Wheeler v. Annesley* (1957), 11 D.L.R. (2d) 573.

"The right of the majority of the members to control the action of the meeting cannot be questioned." *American Aberdeen-Angus Breeders Assn. v. Fullerton*, 325 Ill. 323, 156 N.E. 314 (1927).

resolution is not:

- — *ultra vires* of the company;
- — inconsistent with the constitution;[19]
- — a fraud on the minority;[20]
- — oppressive on the minority;[21]
- — obtained by a trick;[22]
- — one that improperly deprives the company of property belonging to it.[23]

> *Comment:* Most resolutions require a simple majority, some require two-thirds, some require more. (See Rules 106, 107, 108).

7. Right to attend, shareholders

Every person having the right to vote has the right to attend all meetings of holders of securities of his class and of such other classes as the governing statute or the constitution permits or requires.

> *Comment:* It is preferable for the different classes of shareholders to meet separately and vote separately.[24]

8. Right to be heard

Every person having the right to vote has the right to speak and be heard.

> *Comment:* The views of the minority must not be stifled by the majority. The majority may rule, but they have no right to make up their minds without consulting the minority and giving them the opportunity to be heard.[26]

---

[19] *Burland v. Earle,* [1902] A.C. 83; *Brown v. Can-Erin Mines Ltd.* (1960), 25 D.L.R. (2d) 250.

[20] *Menier v. Hooper's Telegraph Works* (1874), 9 Ch. App. 350; *Brown v. Can-Erin Mines Ltd.* (1960), 25 D.L.R. (2d) 250; *Nocton v. Ashburton,* [1914] A.C. 932; *Gray v. Yellowknife Gold Mines Ltd. and Bear Exploration & Radium Ltd.,* [1948] 1 D.L.R. 74.

[21] "The oppression of a majority is detestable and odious; the oppression of a minority is only by one degree less detestable and odious", Gladstone, House of Commons (1870). *Charlebois v. Bienvenu* (1967), 64 D.L.R. (2d) 683; *Scottish Co-operative Wholesale Society Ltd. v. Meyer,* [1958] W.L.R. 404; *Shuttleworth v. Cox Bros. and Co. (Maidenhead), Ltd.,* [1927] 2 K.B. 9; *Re Leigh; Royal Trust Co. v. Norrie,* [1951] 3 D.L.R. 561; *Waddell v. Ontario Canning Co.* (1889), 18 O.R. 41.

[22] *Re Pacific Coast Coal Mines Ltd.,* [1926] 4 D.L.R. 759.

[23] *Cook v. Deeks* (1916), 27 D.L.R. 1; *McGill Shipbuilding & Transportation Co. v. Canadian Bank of Commerce,* [1925] 2 D.L.R. 1183; *Stanishewski v. Tkchuk,* [1955] 4 D.L.R. 517.

[24] Rules 27, 28.

[26] *Const v. Harris* (1824), Turn. & R. 496, 37 E.R. 1191; *Wall v. London & Northern Assets Corp.,* [1898] 2 Ch. 469.

9. Adequate room

Every person having the right to vote has the right to be provided with adequate accommodation for the meeting, with access, adequate light, heat, ventilation, comfort and safety. It is the duty of the chairman to make such provisions.

> *Comment:* The failure to receive these accommodations gives each voter the right to raise a question of privilege (Rule 95).

10. Strangers

Only persons having the right to vote and the company's auditors[27] are entitled to be present at meetings of shareholders. Strangers may be admitted only with the consent of the meeting.

> *Comment:* The presence of persons not entitled to be present may, if objected to, render the proceedings invalid,[28] but if no objection to their presence is taken, the meeting is not thereby invalidated.[29]

11. Interpretation

All matters concerning company meetings are governed by the statute under which the company was incorporated as interpreted by the law of the place of incorporation.[30]

---

[27] See Rules 28, 44, 50, 51, 52, 188.

[28] *Murphy v. Moncton Hospital* (1917), 36 D.L.R. 792; *Harris v. English Canadian Co.* (1905), 3 W.L.R. 5; *Lane v. Norman* (1891), 61 LJ. Ch. 149.

[29] *Carruth v. Imperial Chemical Industries Ltd.*, [1937] A.C. 707.

[30] "The interpretation of those articles [under which the company is constituted] and the operation of them, having regard to the general law, must be governed by the *lex loci contractus* (see *per* Lord Wrenbury in *Russian Commercial & Industrial Bank v. Comptoir d'Escompte de Mulhouse*, [1925] A.C. 112 at p. 149), *i.e.*, by the law from time to time prevailing at the place where the corporate home (domicilio social) was set up", *per* Clauson, L.J., in *Banco de Bilbao v. Sancha*, [1938] 2 K.B. 176 at pp. 194-5; see also *Re Zimmerman and Commonwealth International Leverage Fund Ltd. et al.*, (1966) 58 D.L.R. (2d) 160.

All matters concerning the constitution of a corporation are governed by the law of the place of incorporation (*National Bank of Greece and Athens S.A. v. Metliss*, (1958] A.C. 509).

"It follows that the instrument of incorporation and the laws of a corporation's domicile governed not only its creation and continuing existence, but also all matters of internal management, . . ." (*National Trust Co. Ltd. v. Ebro Irrigation & Power Co. Ltd.; National Trust Co. Ltd. v. Catalonian Land Co. Ltd.*, [1954] 3 D.L.R. 326).

"The charter of a company is the same abroad as it is at home. Where authorized to do business in other jurisdictions, it is still subject to the law of the home of its creation, though it must comply wih the local laws of such other jurisdictions" (*Spitz v. Secretary of State of Canada*, [1939] Ex.C.R. 162) followed in *Brown, Gow, Wilson v. Beleggings-Societeit N.V.* (1961), 29 D.L.R. (2d) 673.

Comment: In a federally incorporated corporation, a Court in Prince Edward Island (where the head office was located) can not interfere with an order of a Quebec Court (where a meeting was called).[31]

ANNUAL MEETINGS

12. Annual meetings of shareholders

Every company statute requires the holding of an annual meeting of shareholders. The business transacted at annual meetings includes:

1. Receiving the financial statements;

2. Reading the auditor's report (where required by statute);

3. Electing directors;

4. Appointing auditors;

5. Confirming bylaws, special bylaws, special resolutions and other acts of the board since the last annual meeting (if proper notice has been given or is waived).

Comment: Annual and special meetings may be held together if the proper notice has been given. (See Rule 38.)

SPECIAL MEETINGS

13. Special meetings of shareholders

Special meetings are meetings called for special purposes.

Comment: Special meetings are sometimes called general, special general or extraordinary meetings.[32] They may be held before, during or after the holding of an annual meeting.

REQUISITIONED MEETINGS

14. Right to call requisitioned meeting

Where by statute the holders of a specified percentage of the issued shares have the right to requisition the board of directors to

---

[31] *Re Zimmerman and Commonwealth International Leverage Fund Ltd. et al.,* (1966) 58 D.L.R. (2d) 160.

[32] *Austin Mining Co. v. Gemmell* (1886), 10 O.R. 696 (C.A.) 703.

call a special meeting,[33] and the directors, including de facto directors,[34] fail to do so, the requisitioning shareholders may convene the meeting.[35]

> *Comment:* If the notice does not specifically set out the statutory authority under which the meeting is being called and observe the conditions precedent as required by the statute, it may nevertheless be valid.[36]

15. Notice for requisitioned meeting

Whether the requisitioned meeting is called by the board or by the shareholders, the length of notice, and the persons served must comply with the statute and the bylaws,[37] and the purposes of the meeting must be clearly defined and specified.[38]

16. Signing notice for requisitioned meeting

The notice for a requisitioned meeting of shareholders ought to be signed by all the requisitionists.

> *Comment:* The notice may still be valid if the documents accompanying it clearly indicate that the meeting is in fact called by all the requisitionists,[39] although not signed by all of them.

COURT-CALLED MEETINGS

17. Power to call meeting

Where the Court[40] is given authority to convene a meeting of shareholders under certain circumstances, it is not necessary to go through the procedure of calling a meeting if such meeting would be futile. The powers of the Court are discretionary.[41]

---

33 *Business Corporations Act,* S.O. 1982, Sections 105 and 106; *Goldhar v. D'Aragon Mines Ltd.* (1977) 15 O.R. (2d) 80.

34 *Streit v. Swanson* [1946] O.R. 565.

35 *Austin Mining Co. v. Gemmel* (1886) 10 O.R. 696 (C.A.) 703.

36 *Isle of Wight Ry. Co. v. Tahourdin* (1883) 25 Ch. D. 329.

37 *Gold-Rex Kirkland Mines Ltd. v. Morrow* [1946] O.R. 415, 418; *Sovereen Mitt, Glove and Robe Co. v. Whitside* (1906) 12 O.L.R. 638.

38 *Austin Mining Co. v. Gemmel* (1886) 10 O.R. 696 (C.A.) 703.

39 *Dalex Mines Ltd. v. Schmidt* (1973) 37 D.L.R. (3d) 17, 5 W.W.R. 357.

40 *Re Zimmerman and Commonwealth International Leverage Fund Ltd. et al.,* (1966) 58 D.L.R. (2d) 160; *Athabasca Holdings Ltd. v. E.N.A. Data-systems Inc.* 30 O.R. (2d) 527; *Re Canadian Javelin Ltd.* 69 D.L.R. (3d) 439.

41 *Re Morris Funeral Holdings Ltd.* (1960) O.W.N. 160 (C.A.); *Re Routley's Holdings Ltd.* (1957) O.W.N. 161 (C.A.).

18. Business at Court-called meetings

Where by statute[42] or otherwise, a meeting is called by the Court, only such business may be conducted which could lawfully be conducted if the meeting had been otherwise convened.[43]

> *Comment:* The enabling section of the statute[44] does not authorize the conduct of any business at a meeting convened by order of the Court which could not lawfully be conducted if the meeting had been otherwise convened.[43]

BOARD MEETINGS

19. Board meetings

Directors can exercise their powers only at duly convened meetings of the board.[45] They act only in their collective capacity,[46] not as individuals.[47] Unless the statute permits them to do so, they cannot appoint substitutes[48] to act for them at board meetings.

> *Comment:* One director cannot constitute a meeting of the board.[49] In the absence of a specific provision in the statute or the constitution, a resolution assented to by all the directors not assembled at a meeting (e.g., by telephone) is not an official act of the corporation.[50] However, some statutes now permit meetings to be held by telephone or other electronic facilities.[51]

---

[42] *Business Corporations Act*, S.O. 1982, Section 106.

[43] *Re: British International Finance (Canada) Ltd., Charlebois et al. v. Bienvenue et al.*, [1968] (2) O.R. 217.

[44] See table inside back cover.

[45] Convened by formal notice, unanimous waiver or consent of absent directors, or immediately following an annual meeting of shareholders (if permitted by the constitution).

[46] "Before directors can meet as such to transact the business of their company they must meet in person . . . , and there must be an agreement, express or implied, to meet in that capacity and not otherwise." (*Harris v. English Canadian Co.*, (1905), 3 W.L.R. 5). See also *Toronto Brewing & Malting Co. v. Blake* (1882), 2 O.R. 175; *Barron v. Potter*, [1914] 1 Ch. 895.

[47] Individual assents are not equivalent to the assent of a meeting. The company is entitled to the protection afforded by a duly convened meeting, and by a resolution properly considered, carried and duly recorded. (*Gray & Farr Ltd. v. Carlile*, [1932] 1 D.L.R. 391.)

[48] *McGuire & Forester Ltd. v. Cadzow*, [1933] 1 D.L.R. 192; *Re Portuguese Consolidated Copper Mines, Ltd.* (1889), 42 Ch. D. 160.

[49] *Re Cowichan Leader Ltd.* (1963), 45 W.W.R. 57; *Re D. & S. Drug Co.* (1916), 10 W.W.R. 612, rev'd on other grounds 31 D.L.R. 643.

[50] *Re Associated Color Laboratories Ltd.*, 12 D.L.R. (3d) 338.

[51] *Business Corporations Act*, S.O. 1982, c. 4, Section 126(13).

20. Right to attend, directors

Every director has the right to attend and participate in all meetings of the board of directors.[52] He cannot be excluded from meetings of the board.[53]

> *Comment:* Unless permitted by the statute, directors cannot be represented by proxy[54] or substitute. A director can enforce his rights to be present and vote at meetings of the board.

21. Annual meetings of the board

At the meeting of the board prior to the calling of an annual meeting of shareholders, the board considers and approves the financial statements, appoints two members to sign them to indicate the board's approval, fixes a date and place for the annual meeting, approves the notice of meeting, form of proxy (if there is to be a proxy solicitation) and an information circular (if the corporation is a public offering corporation).

> *Comment:* In some jurisdictions sending a form of proxy is mandatory.

22. Notice of meetings of the board

In the absence of provisions to the contrary in the governing statute or the constitution, notice of the time and place of meetings of the board of directors must be given to all directors, otherwise the business transacted thereat is invalid.[55] Notice of business to be transacted at meetings of the board is not necessary in the absence of special provisions to the contrary in the articles or bylaws.[56] If permitted by the constitution, no notice is required for the first meeting of the board of directors held immediately following the annual meeting for the purpose of electing and appointing officers,[57] if all the directors are present or have waived notice.

---

[52] *Boak v. Woods* [1926] 1 D.L.R. 1186.

[53] *Hayes v. Bristol Plant Hire* [1957] 1 All E.R. 685; *Howard v. Dench* [1942] 2 D.L.R. 177 (B.C.C.A.).

[54] *Re Portuguese Consolidated Copper* (1889) 42 Ch. D. 160.

[55] *Wills v. Murray* (1850), 4 Exch. 843.

[56] As directors are the select managing body of the company, notice of special business is not a prerequisite to the proceedings being valid (*La Compagnie de Mayville v. Whitley,* [1896] 1 Ch. 788). See Rule 23.

[57] The tenure of office of officers expires with the re-election of the directors. It is therefore advisable to elect/appoint officers as soon as possible after the election of directors (*Ghimpelman v. Bercovici,* [1957] S.C.R. 128).

Comment: If due notice is not sent to all directors the meeting is invalid unless the absent director waives notice or acquiesces to the transaction of business.

23. Waiver of notice by directors

A director may waive notice of a meeting of the board[58] and any irregularities in connection with the convening of the meeting, either in writing or by attending and participating without objection.[59] No notice is required for a meeting of the board of directors if all the directors attend and participate without objection.

Comment: Strangers may not be admitted without the consent of the meeting.

24. Director's right to vote

A director cannot vote on a motion at a board meeting if he is personally interested in the motion[60] unless the statute or the constitution specifically provides otherwise. In any case he must make full disclosure of his interest.

Comment: At a shareholders meeting a shareholder who is a director is not under the same restrictions.[61] (See Rule 157.)

25. Quorum—board meeting

Unless fixed otherwise by the statute or the constitution, the number of directors constituting a quorum for meetings of the board is a majority.

26. Chairman—board meetings

The chairman of the board, if present and willing, shall preside at meetings of the board. In the absence or refusal of the chairman to preside, or to continue presiding, the president shall preside, unless the constitution provides otherwise.[62] If the chair-

---

[58] See Rule 4.

[59] *Société Coopérative Agricole v. Tardiff* [1944] Que. S.C. 269.

[60] *Garvie v. Axmith, supra; Transvaal Lands Co. v. New Belgium (Transvaal) Land & Development Co.*, [1914] 2 Ch. 488; *Gray v. Yellowknife Gold Mines Ltd. and Bear Exploration & Radium Ltd.*, [1948] 1 D.L.R. 473. The transaction may be confirmed by the shareholders, *Business Corporations Act* (Ontario), 1982, Sec. 132(8).

[61] *Great Western Garment v. M.N.R.* [1948] 1 D.L.R. 225; *North-West Transportation Co. Ltd. v. Beatty* (1887), 12 App. Cas. 589; *Burland v. Earle,* (1902) A.C. 83; *Goodfellow v. Nelson Line (Liverpool), Ltd.*, [1912] 2 Ch. 324.

[62] See Rule 62.

man is disqualified from voting or disqualifies himself by his actions, the board may elect a new chairman from among the directors.[63]

> *Comment:* Calling the meeting does not give the chairman any additional rights.[64] For secretary of board meetings, see Rules 73 to 75.

CLASS MEETINGS

27. Class meetings—separate

Meetings of holders of different classes of shares should be held separately.

> *Comment:* "In my opinion the better and wiser course is to make provision for the holding of truly separate meetings in the ordinary way, even at the risk of inconvenience."[65] The mere presence of members of another class may impair freedom of discussion and is therefore undesirable.

28. Class meetings—notice

Where the rights of a class of security holders are affected, they should receive notice of the meeting even though they may have no right to vote thereat.[66]

> *Comment:* The conditions attached to preference or special shares usually provide for notice of such meetings.[67]

EXECUTIVE COMMITTEE MEETINGS

29. Electing a chairman

In the absence of specific provisions in the bylaw authorizing the executive committee[68] and in the resolution creating it, the committee shall appoint from among its members, a chairman.[69]

---

63 See Rule 65.

64 *Gray v. Yellowknife Gold Mines Ltd.* [1946] O.W.N. 938.

65 Lord Maugham in *Carruth v. Imperial Chemical Industries* [1937] A.C. 707; *Re Langley's Ltd.*, [1938] O.R. 123; *Re Second Standard Royalties Ltd.* (1930), 66 O.L.R. 288.

66 *Sovereign Life Assurance Co. v. Dodd* (1892) 2 Q.B. 573.

67 *Re: MacKenzie & Co., Ltd.*, [1916] 2 Ch. 450.

68 The size and composition of the executive committee is fixed by statute.

69 In accordance with Rule 64.

30. Quorum for executive committee

If no quorum has been fixed, the committee shall fix a quorum comprising not less than a majority of its members.

31. Minutes of executive committee meetings

The committee shall appoint a secretary of the executive committee who shall keep minutes of each meeting. Minutes of every meeting of the executive committee must be filed with board of directors forthwith.

32. Vacancies

The executive committee has no power to fill vacancies or to appoint additional members.[70]

33. Audit Committee

Rules of order for meetings of the audit committee[71] are the same as for meetings of the executive committee.

---

[70] *Re Liverpool Household Stores* (1890) 59 L.J. Ch. 616; *Cook v. Ward* (1877) 2 C.P.D. 255 (C.A.).

[71] The size and composition of the audit committee is fixed by statute.

CHAPTER II

NOTICE OF MEETINGS

GENERALLY

34. Essentials of a valid notice

In the absence of special provisions in the constitution,[1] notices of meetings of shareholders must:

— give adequate length of notice;

— show date, time and place of the meeting;

— be issued on proper authority;

— set out nature of business[2] to be conducted;

— be served on every person entitled to receive notice.

---

[1] Memorandum of association and articles or letters patent and bylaws. See also applicable securities legislation.

[2] The business to be transacted at any meeting of shareholders must be specified in the notice, *Re British Sugar Refining Co.* (1857), 3 K. & J. 408, 69 E.R. 1168; *Smith v. Paringa Mines Ltd.*, [1906] 2 Ch. 193; *McDougall v. Black Lake Asbestos & Chrome Ltd.* (1920), 47 O.L.R. 328; *Lumbers v. Fretz*, [1928] 4 D.L.R. 269, 854.

35. Form of notice

Notices are not expected to follow a rigid form,[3] but they must specify the business to be conducted with clearness and accuracy.[4] A notice must be read and construed as an ordinary businessman would read and construe it.

> *Comment:* The court does not scrutinize these notices with a view to criticizing them or finding defects, but looks at them fairly.[5] One notice convening two meetings may be valid (Rule 61).[6]

NATURE OF BUSINESS

36. Business in full

All the motions (resolutions) and other business intended to be presented to the meeting must be set out in the notice[7] either in full or in sufficient detail to give the full effect thereof clearly and accurately.

> *Comment:* Notice that the motion proposed to be passed may be seen at the head office is not sufficient.[8] A general intimation is not enough. The directors should take the shareholders into their confidence and tell them what they propose to do.[9] Notice of a meeting to authorize remuneration to be given must set this out clearly.[10] Failure to set out business in full may invalidate the notice, the proxies and the business conducted.

---

[3] See Conditional Notices (Rule 60).

[4] *Zimmerman v. Trustee of Andrew Motherwell of Canada Ltd.* [1925] 3 W.W.R. 42.

[5] "I think the question may be put in this form: 'What is the meaning which this notice would fairly carry to ordinary minds?' That, I think, is the reasonable test." (Chitty, J., in *Henderson v. Bank of Australasia* (1890), 45 Ch. D. 330, at p. 337.)

[6] *Re Jenner Institute of Preventive Medicine* (1899), 15 T.L.R. 394.

[7] The resolution need not be set out in full but the business to be conducted must be set out clearly and accurately. "The failure to specify the business with clearness and accuracy will, of course, invalidate the notice and render the meeting irregular." (*Zimmerman v. Trustee of Andrew Motherwell of Canada Ltd.* (1923), 54 O.L.R. 342; aff'd (1925) 3 D.L.R. 953.)

[8] *Normandy v. Ind. Coope & Co. Ltd.*, [1908] 1 Ch. 84.

[9] The directors should tell the shareholders that they propose to confer on the directors larger powers and larger remuneration. (*Normandy v. Ind, Coope & Co. Ltd., supra*).

[10] *Baillie v. Oriental Telephone and Electric Co., Ltd.*, [1915] 1 Ch. 503.

37. Full disclosure

In addition to setting out in full the motions (resolutions) intended to be presented to the meeting,[11] the notice must (unless the motions are self-explanatory) give the background and other data necessary for the shareholder to be able to determine for himself whether or not he should attend or whether or not he should appoint a proxyholder.[12] The purposes as set out in the notice and in any accompanying or following information circulars or solicitations must be complete, accurate, clear, and free from trickery.[13]

> *Comment:* If the notice does not conform with this rule, the notice and the meeting may be declared irregular.[14] (Rules 55, 56 and 57.) Notices are not construed with excessive strictness but as an ordinary businessman would understand them.[15]

38. Special business

Special business may be transacted at annual meetings of shareholders if proper notice of the special business has been given.[16] The same notice may convene an annual meeting at which

---

[11] *Garvie v. Axmith* (1961), 31 D.L.R. (2d) 65; *Re National Grocers Co. Ltd.*, [1938] 3 D.L.R. 106; *Pacific Coast Coal Mines Ltd. v. Arbuthnot* (1917), 36 D.L.R. 564; *Re Dorman, Long & Co. Ltd.; Re South Durham Steel & Iron Co. Ltd.*, [1934] 1 Ch. 635; *Re N. Slater Co. Ltd.*, [1947] 2 D.L.R. 311; *Liquidators of Imperial Mercantile Credit Ass'n v. Coleman and Knight* (1873), L.R. 6 H.L. 189; See *Victors Ltd. v. Lingard*, [1927] 1 Ch. 323.

[12] Controlling shareholders can still sell assets of the company to their own subsidiaries provided that full and fair disclosure is made to all shareholders of what is being done and all shareholders are treated alike. (*Wotherspoon v. Canadian Pacific* 35 O.R. (2d) 449); *Goldex Mines Ltd. v. Revill* (1974) 7 O.R. (2d) 216; *Garvie v. Axmith* [1962] O.R. 65;

Failure to set out in the notice an agreement which the shareholders were asked to ratify at the meeting invalidated the proxies sent in and the votes taken thereon, and the agreement was set aside (*Pacific Coast Coal Mines Ltd. v. Arbuthnot, supra*; *Lumbers v. Fretz*, [1928] 4 D.L.R. 269, aff'd [1929] 1 D.L.R. 51; *MacConnell v. E. Prill & Co. Ltd.*, [1916] 2 Ch. 57). See also *Normandy v. Ind, Coope & Co. Ltd.*, [1908] 1 Ch. 84.

[13] *Kaye v. Croydon Tramways Co.*, [1898] 1 Ch. 358; *Tiessen v. Henderson*, [1899] 1 Ch. 861; *Baillie v. Oriental Telephone and Electric Co., Ltd.*, [1915] 1 Ch. 503.

[14] *Wills v. Murray* (1850), 4 Exch. 843; *Lumbers v. Fretz*, [1928] 4 D.L.R. 269, 854, aff'd [1929] 1 D.L.R. 51; *Kaye v. Croydon Tramways Co., supra*; *Tiessen v. Henderson, supra*; *Jackson v. Munster Bank* (1884), 13 L.R. Ir. 118; *Pelech v. Ukrainian Mutual Benefit Ass'n of Saint Nicholas of Canada*, [1940] 4 D.L.R. 342.

[15] *Alexander v. Simpson* (1889), 43 Ch. D. 139; *Irvin v. Irvin Porcupine Gold Mines Ltd. and Mulliette*, [1940] 3 D.L.R. 785 *n*.

[16] *McDougall v. Blake Lake Asbestos & Chrome Co. Ltd.* (1920), 47 O.L.R. 328; *Christopher v. Noxon* (1883), 4 O.R. 672; *Re Clark, Shimmin v. Clark*, [1932] 3 D.L.R. 702; *Graham v. Van Diemen's Land Co.* (1856), 1 H. & N. 541, 156 E.R. 1316.

special business may be conducted or both annual and special meetings to be held consecutively.[17]

LENGTH OF NOTICE
39. Time of notice

In the absence of special provisions in the constitution,[18] notice of meetings of shareholders must be mailed, in the case of a public offering company, at least 21 clear days and in the case of a private company, at least 10 clear days before the date of the meeting, to the shareholder's last address as shown on the books of the company.[19]

> *Comment:* If the governing statute or the constitution does not call for a specific number of days' notice, the number must be reasonable,[20] and if the constitution does call for a specific number of days' notice, the number of days must be "clear", excluding both the day of service or mailing and the day on which the meeting is to be held.[21] Fractions of days are not counted.

40. Insufficient time

If the required number of days' notice for a meeting has not been given (unless all persons entitled thereto have waived or received notice) the meeting is invalid and all business transacted thereat is a nullity. The proxies for such a meeting are invalid.[22]

41. Meeting cannot be postponed

Once a notice of a meeting of shareholders (or of the board) has been given, it cannot be recalled. The meeting cannot be postponed by another notice.[23]

> *Comment:* The meeting must actually be convened and then adjourned in the regular manner.

---

[17] *Re Jenner Institute of Preventive Medicine* (1899) 15 T.L.R. 394.

[18] *Courchêne v. Viger Park Co.* (1915), 23 D.L.R. 693.

[19] In Ontario not less than 21 days' notice must be given in the case of an offering company, and in the case of other companies, not less than 10 days.

[20] *R. v. Hill* (1825), 4 B. & C. 426, 107 E.R. 1118.

[21] *Ashton v. Powers,* (1921), 67 D.L.R. 222; *Re Hector Whaling Ltd.,* [1936] Ch. 208. "An interval of time not less than fourteen days is equivalent to saying that fourteen days must intervene or elapse between the two dates" (Chitty, J., in *Re Railway Sleepers Supply Co.* (1885), 29 Ch. D. 204). Subject to any special provisions the length of notice must allow a sufficient margin of time for delivery of the letter (*Ashton v. Powers, supra*).

[22] Rule 3; *Melville v. Graham-Yooll* [1936] Scots Law Times News 54; *John Morley Buildup v. Barras* [1891] 2 Ch. 386; *In re Hector Whaling Ltd.* [1936] 1 Ch. 208; *Ashton v. Powers* (1922) 51 O.L.R. 309.

[23] *Smith v. Paringa Mines Ltd.,* [1906] 2 Ch. 193.

42. Notice of adjourned meeting of shareholders

When a meeting of shareholders is adjourned to a fixed date to complete unfinished business, another notice is unnecessary,[24] but no new business not covered in the original notice may be transacted unless a new and proper notice is given.[25] When the meeting is adjourned for a period longer than the time required for notices of meeting, a notice of the adjournment is required, unless the constitution provides otherwise.

> *Comment:* Under the new Ontario *Business Corporations Act* (S.O. 1982, c. 4, *Section* 95(3)) if a meeting of shareholders is adjourned for less than 30 days, it is not necessary (unless the bylaws so provide) to give notice of the adjourned meeting.

PROPER AUTHORITY

43. Authority

The notice must be signed by the person or persons having authority under the statute or the constitution to convene meetings.[26] Such authority may be given subsequently.[27]

> *Comment:* If the authority is given to the board of directors, the directors must act as a board; one director or one officer or even a quorum of the directors will not suffice,[28] but the board may direct the secretary to sign the notice on behalf of the board. A notice signed by a shareholder is a nullity,[29] even after all the directors have resigned, except

---

24 *Wills v. Murray* (1850) 4 Exch. 843.

25 *R. v. Grimshaw* (1847), 10 Q.B. 747, 116 E.R. 284; *Kerr v. Wilkie* (1860), 1 L.T. 501; *McLaren v. Thomson*, [1917] 2 Ch. 261; *Wills v. Murray, supra; Spencer v. Kennedy*, [1926] 1 Ch. 125; *Neuschild v. British Equatorial Oil Co. Ltd.*, [1925] 1 Ch. 346; *Christopher v. Noxon* (1883), 4 O.R. 672.

26 *E.g.*, the board of directors, any two directors, ten per cent of the shareholders, any officer, the president, the secretary, etc. as the case may be.

27 A notice issued by the secretary without the authority of a resolution of the board duly made is invalid, but the notice can be adopted and ratified by resolution passed at a proper meeting of the board prior to the shareholders' meeting (*Re Haycraft Gold Reduction & Mining Co., supra; Harben v. Phillips* (1882), 23 Ch. D. 14; *Hooper v. Kerr, Stuart & Co. Ltd.* (1900), 83 L.T. 729). "The question is whether, although the notice was not authorized beforehand, it has been so ratified now as to make it a good and valid notice. In my opinion it has. The principle of the cases is that the ratification of an act purporting to be done by an agent on your behalf dates back to the performance of the act." (*Hooper v. Kerr, Stuart & Co., Ltd., supra.*) See also *Morris v. Kanssen*, [1946] A.C. 459.

28 *Re Haycraft Gold Reduction & Mining Co.*, [1900] 2 Ch. 230; *Courchêne v. Viger Park Co.* (1915), 23 D.L.R. 693; *Beauchemin v. Beauchemin & Sons Ltd.* (1926), 64 Que. S.C. 300; *Marley King Line Const. Ltd. v. Marley*, [1963] O.R. 302.

29 *South Shore Development v. Snow*, 19 D.L.R. (3d) 601 (1973), 4 NSR (2d) 601.

in the case of a requisitioned meeting (Rule 16), or in the case of a meeting to fill a vacancy in the board under Section 124(3) of the *Business Corporations Act* (Ontario) 1982.

44. Responsibility of signer

The party who signs the notice must assure himself that he is property authorized to sign.

> *Comment:* Ordinarily notices are signed "By order of board" or "On behalf of the board" over the signature of the secretary. The secretary should assure himself that he has authority for signing.

> *Forms:* "By order of the board", *per* S. . . . Secretary; "By order of the president", *per* S; "By D . . . and F . . . directors of the Company"; "By L, M, N, O, & P, holding ten per cent or more of the common shares of the company."

TIME AND PLACE

45. Date of meeting

The date fixed for the meeting must be an ordinary business day and one reasonably convenient for the voters to attend.[30] It must not be a holiday.[31]

46. Time of meeting

Meetings are to be held within normal business hours. The hour must be fixed and unless otherwise indicated is to be official local time.

---

[30] Directors should not fix a date or any hour for holding the meeting of shareholders for the purpose of preventing the shareholders or any of them from exercising their voting powers. An injunction was granted to prevent the holding of an early meeting in July instead of in August as usual which was purposely designed to prevent a group of shareholders from voting newly acquired shares (*Cannon v. Trask* (1875), L.R. 20 Eq. 669).

[31] Under the Interpretation Act, R.S.O. 1980, c. 219, s. 30, "holiday" includes Sunday, New Year's Day, Good Friday, Easter Monday, Christmas Day, the birthday, or the day fixed by proclamation of the Governor General for the celebration of the birthday of the reigning Sovereign, Victoria Day, Dominion Day, Labour Day, Remembrance Day, and any day appointed by proclamation of the Governor General or the Lieutenant Governor as a public holiday or for a general fast or thanksgiving, and when any holiday, except Remembrance Day, falls on a Sunday, the day next following is in lieu thereof a holiday.

A Quebec case held that it was not illegal to hold a meeting on Ascension Day in the absence of specific statutory prohibition (*Nesbitt Thompson & Co. Ltd. v. McColl Frontenac Oil Co. Ltd.* (1938), 43 Que. P.R. 138).

Comment: If one meeting is to be held immediately after another meeting convened for the same day and place, the estimated time of the second meeting should be given, or the words "immediately following the . . . meeting"[32] should be added. If daylight saving time is in existence, the notice should indicate whether standard or daylight saving time is intended. Calling a meeting to be held before 9:00 a.m. or after 4:00 p.m. may be considered oppressive under some circumstances.

47. Place of meeting

Meetings of shareholders and of directors must be held at the place where the head office of the company is situated unless the governing statute or constitution authorize other places where the meeting may be held.

Comment: The word "place" has a geographical significance.[33] The meeting may be held anywhere within the geographical area in which the head office is located, unless the constitution provides otherwise.

PERSONS ENTITLED TO NOTICE

48. Persons entitled to notice

All persons entitled to vote at the meeting[34] are entitled to be given notice. If the notice is not properly served on every person so entitled, the meeting is irregular and the proceedings invalid.[35] Public offering companies also require information circulars to be sent, as well as, in some cases, proxy solicitation materials.[36]

---

[32] *Carruth v. Imperial Chemical Industries, Ltd.,* [1937] A.C. 707, at p. 760.

[33] *Re Routley's Holdings Ltd.* (1960) 22 D.L.R. (2d) 410; see also *Re Zimmerman and Commonwealth Leverage Fund Ltd. et al.* (1960) 58 D.L.R. (2d) 160.

[34] Some statutes also require that the auditor be notified of meetings of shareholders. (See table inside back cover.)

[35] *Anderson Lumber v. Canadian Conifer* 66 D.L.R. (3d) 553; 77 D.L.R. (3d) 126; *R. v. Langhorn* (1836), 4 Ad. & E. 538, 111 E.R. 889; *Alexander v. Simpson* (1889), 43 Ch. D. 139; *Babic v. Milinkovic* 22 D.L.R. (3d) 732; (*Charleboise v. Bienvenue* 64 D.L.R. (2d) 683, (1967) 2 O.R. 635 distinguished).

[36] See Securities Acts and Corporation Acts; *Probe Mines v. Goldex Mines* [1973] 3 O.R. 869; *Garvie v. Axmith* [1962] O.R. 65.

Comment: The fact that the result of the meeting would have been the same, if the person not notified had been present at the meeting, does not excuse failure to give notice.[37] Notice should be given to shareholders who, although not of a class entitled to vote, may be affected by the result of the meeting, as in the case of a meeting called to consider the winding up of the company.[38] Most articles and bylaws contain a provision whereby the inadvertent failure to give notice does not invalidate the meeting.

49. Name on register

Entry in the share register of the name of a person as being the holder of a share is conclusive of his right to vote such share[39] and to be given notice. If the constitution provides for a record date, persons recorded as shareholders after that date are not entitled to notice or to vote.

Comment: As a matter of courtesy, most companies send notices of meetings to persons recorded after the record date, but this does not entitle them to vote.

50. Trustee of shareholder

An executor, administrator, committee of a mentally incompetent person, guardian or trustee of a shareholder is entitled to notice and may vote if he files with the company satisfactory evidence of his appointment.

51. Mortgagee of shares

A mortgagee of shares is entitled to notice if notice of the mortgage is filed with the company and such mortgage expressly empowers the mortgagee to exercise the voting rights on those shares.

37 *Smyth v. Darley* (1849), 2 H.L. Cas. 789; *Re East Norfolk Tramways Co.* (1877), 5 Ch. D. 963; *Longfield Parish Council v. Wright* (1918), 88 L.J. Ch. 119; *Re Hampshire Land Co.* (1896), 2 Ch. 743; *Lane v. Norman* (1891), 61 L.J. Ch. 149; *Smith v. Deighton* (1852), 8 Moo. 179, 14 E.R. 69; *Lawes' Case* (1852), 1 De G.M. & G. 421, 42 E.R. 614; *Young v. Ladies' Imperial Club Ltd.,* [1920] 2 K.B. 523; *R. v. McDonald,* [1913] 2 I.R. 55; *Canada Furniture Co. v. Banning* (1917), 39 D.L.R. 313; *Dobson v. Fussy* (1831), 7 Bing. 305, 131 E.R. 117; *R. v. Hill* (1825), 4 B. & C. 426, 107 E.R. 1118; *R. v. Shrewsbury* (1736), Lee temp. Hard. 147, 95 E.R. 94.
38 *Re East Norfolk Tramways Co.* (1877), 5 Ch. D. 963; *Re United Fuel Investment Ltd.* (July 31, 1961, McLelland, J., unreported).
39 *Dominion Royalty Corp. v. Holborn* (1932), 41 O.W.N. 288; *Tough Oakes Gold Mines Ltd. v. Foster* (1917), 34 D.L.R. 748.

52. Auditor

All notices and other communications relating to meetings of shareholders should be sent to the auditor of the company, who is entitled to attend and be heard at such meetings.

> *Comment:* In some jurisdictions, this is a specific statutory requirement. (See table inside back cover.) It is considered good practice to invite the auditor to all meetings of the shareholders. Auditors are appointed by the shareholders. The information that can be supplied by the auditor and his report is of major significance to the shareholders as a whole, as it is to them that the auditor owes a duty to detect and report on any fraud or gross negligence of management from which the shareholders may suffer damage.[40]

DELIVERY OF NOTICE

53. Method of service

Unless the articles or bylaws provide otherwise, notice may be served on the person entitled to vote personally or by mail at the address shown on the register.

> *Comment:* A notice regularly posted but not received is nevertheless valid.[41] It is preferable, but not essential, to follow the registered address literally. A substantially accurate designation of the registered address is enough.[42] If a shareholder's address is unknown[43] the notice should be mailed to the last known address.

54. Proof of service

The person who delivers or mails the notice proves service thereof by making and filing an affidavit or statutory declaration to that effect (Form 8).

---

[40] *Turner v. Canadian Pacific Ltd.*, (1980) 27 O.R. (2d) 549; see also *Turner and Lewis v. Canadian Pacific Ltd.*, S.C.O. motion of October 19, 1979, appealed and dismissed on consent.

[41] *James v. Chartered Accountants Institute* (1907), 98 L.T. 225.

[42] *Liverpool Marine Ins. Co. v. Haughton* (1874), 23 W.R. 93.

[43] *Dickson v. Halesowen Steel Co.,* [1928] W.N. 33.

NOTICE FAULTY

55. Invalid provisions

A notice of meeting may be wholly[44] or only partially[45] invalid if it contains invalid provisions.

> *Comment:* If only one object of a meeting can legally be done, the possible invalidity of the other objects has no bearing upon it.[46]

56. Inadequate information

Shareholders are entitled to be given sufficient information with particularity about the business to be transacted at the meeting to enable them to reach an intelligent conclusion.[47] If a notice of a meeting of shareholders lacks adequate information or is otherwise improper, the business transacted is a nullity,[48] and the court may order a new meeting to be called. Proxies given for use at such a meeting are invalid.[49]

> *Comment:* Failure to notify shareholders of motions of substance which will be presented may invalidate the meeting, the proxies and the resolutions.[50] (See Rules 36 and 37.) Failure to mail financial statements does not affect the meeting.[51]

---

44 "The order (of the Court) directing the calling of the meeting contained such provisions as to render it invalid. I think the validity of the whole proceedings was vitiated by this unwarrantable notice." (Middleton, J. A., in *Re Dairy Corp. of Canada Ltd.,* [1934] 3 D.L.R. 347, at p. 349.)

45 A notice is not wholly invalid because it extends to something which cannot be done at the meeting (*Cleve v. Financial Corp.* (1873), L.R. 16 Eq. 363).

46 *Zimmerman v. Trustee of Andrew Motherwell of Canada Ltd.* (1923), 54 O.L.R. 342, following *Thomson v. Henderson's Transvaal Estates, Ltd.,* [1908] 1 Ch. 765; *Re British Sugar Refining Co.* (1857), 3 K. & J. 408, 69 E.R. 1168; *Re London and Mediterranean Bank, Ltd., Wright's Case* (1871), 7 Ch. App. 55.

47 *Rudkin v. British Columbia Automobile* 70 W.W.R. 649.

48 *Garvie v. Axmith* (1962) O.R. 65; *Jamieson v. Hotel Renfrew Trustees* [1941] 4 D.L.R. 470; *Gold-Rex Kirkland Mines Ltd. v. Morrow* (1944) O.R. 415; *Zimmerman v. Trustee of Andrew Motherwell of Canada Ltd.* (1925) 3 W.W.R. 42 (P.C.P.).

49 *Lumbers v. Fretz* [1928] 4 D.L.R. 269, 854, aff'd [1929] 1 D.L.R. 51.

50 *Pacific Coast Coal Mines Ltd. v. Arbuthnot* (1917), 36 D.L.R. 564; *Lumbers v. Fretz,* [1928] 4 D.L.R. 269, 854, aff'd [1929] 1 D.L.R. 51; *MacConnell v. E. Prill & Co. Ltd.,* [1916] 2 Ch. 57; *Re Lemay Ltd.* (1924), 26 O.W.N. 443; *Re Bridport Old Brewery Co.* (1867), 2 Ch. App. 191. See also *Cannon v. Toronto Corn Exchange* (1879), 27 Gr. 23, aff'd 5 O.A.R. 268; *Milot v. Pereault* (1886), 12 Q.L.R. 193; *Longfield Parish Council v. Wright* (1918), 88 L.J. Ch. 119; *Young v. Ladies' Imperial Club, Ltd.,* [1920] 2 K.B. 523; *R. v. McDonald,* [1913] 2 I.R. 55; *Dolly Varden Mines Ltd. v. Sunshine Exploration Ltd.* 64 D.L.R. (2d) 283.

51 *Watt v. Commonwealth Petroleum Ltd.,* [1938] 4 D.L.R. 701. See also *Bayshore Investments Limited v. Endako Mines Ltd.* [1971] 2 W.W.R. 622.

57. Business not mentioned

Important business not mentioned in the notice convening a meeting of shareholders cannot be transacted.[52] If such business is conducted at a meeting, it may be declared null, but this will not render the whole meeting irregular.[53]

> *Comment:* When special business is intended to be transacted at an annual meeting, special notice must be given. Within limits, the business of which notice was given may be varied,[54] but the meeting cannot go beyond the purposes for which it was called.

WAIVER OF NOTICE

58. By shareholders

Shareholders may at any time waive notice of a meeting and any irregularities in connection with the convening of a meeting of shareholders. By attending and participating in the meeting, without objecting, shareholders may be deemed to have waived notice.[55]

> *Comment:* This does not apply if all members are present by accident in one place and objection is taken to considering it a meeting.[56]

59. By proxyholders

Proxyholders, if authorized by the documents appointing them, may waive notice of meetings and any irregularities in connection with the convening of the meeting[57] for which they were appointed.

[52] See Rule 36. *Irvin v. Irvin Porcupine* [1940] O.W.N. 315; *McDougall v. Blake Lake Asbestos* (1920) 47 O.L.R. 328; *Longfield Parish Council v. Wright* (1918), 88 L.J. Ch. 119. Failure to mention ratification of bylaw increasing number of directors as a purpose of the meeting renders the notice defective. (*Gray v. Yellowknife Gold Mines Ltd. and Bear Exploration & Radium Ltd.,* [1945] O.R. 688).

[53] *Re Second Standard Royalties Ltd.* (1930), 66 O.R. 288; *Re British Sugar Refining Co.* (1857), 3 K. of J. 408, 69 E.R. 1168.

[54] A notice of meeting for the voluntary winding up of a company and the appointment of W as liquidator is proper where the meeting approved the winding up but appointed M as liquidator (*Bethell v. Trench Tubeless Tyre Co.,* [1900] 1 Ch. 408). Where the notice stated that three named persons would be appointed directors, and, instead, five were appointed, the notice was upheld (*Betts & Co., Ltd. v. McNaghten,* [1910] 1 Ch. 430). Where a notice states that it is proposed to remove any of the directors all may be removed (*Isle of Wight Ry. Co. v. Tahourdin* (1883), 25 Ch. D. 320).

[55] *Eisenberg (Formerly Walton) v. Bank of Nova Scotia and Ridout,* [1965] S.C.R. 681; *Re British Sugar Refining Co., supra; Re Express Engineering Works, Ltd.,* [1920] 1 Ch. 466; *Re Excell Footwear Co.; Ex parte Nova Scotia Trust Co.,* [1923] 3 D.L.R. 212; *Re Oxted Motor Co. Ltd.,* [1921] 3 K.B. 32; *Wenlock (Baroness) v. River Dee Co.* (1887), 36 Ch. D. 674; *Re British Sugar Refining Co., supra; Machell v. Nevinson* (1724), 11 East 84n, 103 E.R. 936.

[56] Rule 2.

[57] *Marks v. Rocsand Co. Ltd.* (1920), 55 D.L.R. 557; rev'd 64 D.L.R. 254.

CONDITIONAL NOTICE

60. Conditional notice of meeting

A notice must not be conditional upon the happening of some event unless such event directly affects the business to be transacted at the meeting.

> *Comment:* A notice that a meeting will be held in the event of a certain contingency not related to the meeting is invalid[58] but a notice given for a meeting to be held in the event that a bylaw is enacted or confirmed at a prior meeting is valid.[59]

61. Alternative resolutions

A notice may suggest alternative motions to be proposed at the same or a subsequent meeting called at the same time.

> *Comment:* A notice of two alternative motions (resolutions), one for the first meeting and the other for the second meeting in the event that the first resolution is not passed, is not invalid.[60]

---

[58] *Alexander v. Simpson* (1889), 43 Ch. D. 139.

[59] A notice issued in anticipation of the passing of a statute enabling the meeting to be held is a valid notice if the statute is passed and is effective on the date of the meeting (*Pacific Coast Coal Mines Ltd. v. Arbuthnot* (1917), 36 D.L.R. 564).

[60] *Tiessen v. Henderson*, [1899] 1 Ch. 861. But see *Alexander v. Simpson, supra.* (See Rule 60.)

CHAPTER III

ORGANIZATION OF MEETINGS

CHAIRMAN

62. Chairman—shareholders meetings

The person who by statute[1] or by the constitution[2] has the right to preside shall preside at all meetings. In the absence of specific provision for a chairman, the president shall preside. In the absence or refusal of the president to preside, or to continue presiding, the vice-president shall preside. The chairman is referred to in the third person by himself and others ("the chair").

> *Comment:* If the constitution provides that the president shall preside and he is present and willing to preside, another person cannot be chairman.[3] Calling a meeting does not include the right to preside at the meeting.[4]

---

[1] See table inside back cover.

[2] See glossary.

[3] *Re Lemay Ltd.* (1924), 26 O.W.N. 443; *Freemont Canning Co. & Johnson v. Wall & Fine Foods of Canada Ltd.*, [1940] 4 D.L.R. 86, aff'd [1941] 3 D.L.R. 96. Where the bylaws provide that the president shall have the general charge and control of the business and affairs of the company he has the right to preside at meetings of shareholders and should refuse to retire from the chair if requested (*Freemont Canning Co. & Johnson v. Wall & Fine Foods, supra*).

[4] *Gray v. Yellowknife Gold Mines Ltd.* [1946] O.W.N. 938.

63. Absence of chairman

In the absence of a provision in the constitution in that regard, if no one having the right to preside is present and willing to preside, a chairman shall be chosen by election or appointment (as required by the constitution) from among those present and entitled to vote. Such chairman should not take the chair until after a wait of fifteen minutes from the time appointed for the holding of the meeting or until the person having the right to preside, refuses to preside or to continue presiding.

64. Election of chairman

To elect a chairman for the meeting, a temporary chairman who is not a candidate for the chair[5] is selected. He asks for nominations and takes a vote.[6] The one receiving the largest number of votes becomes the chairman. If only one is nominated, the temporary chairman asks for a motion that the person nominated be declared elected chairman of the meeting. A voter may not propose himself as chairman but may vote for himself.

> *Comment:* The right to nominate a chairman carries with it the right to remove, whether he was elected or appointed. The words "elected" and "appointed" are synonymous in this connection.[7] Any objection to the election of a chairman must be made at once, otherwise his election is deemed to be valid,[8] but a casting vote cast by an irregularly elected chairman may be questioned.[9]

65. Disqualification

If the chairman disqualifies himself by his actions, the voters may elect a new chairman from among themselves and proceed with the meeting.[10]

---

[5] No man shall preside at his own election and return himself (*R. v. White* (1867), L.R. 2 Q.B. 557). No man shall be a judge in his own cause, as interest constitutes a legal incapacity to a person being a judge (*Fanagan v. Kernan* (1881), 8 L.R. Ir. 44).

[6] Rules 96 to 101.

[7] *Van Alstyne v. Rankin & St. Lawrence Corp. Ltd.* [1952] Que. S.C. 12.

[8] *Cornwall and Pain v. Woods* (1846), 4 Notes of Cases 555.

[9] *Clark v. Workman* (1920) 1 I.R. 107.

[10] *Gray v. Yellowknife Gold Mines Ltd.*, [1946] O.W.N. 938; *Catesby v. Burnett* [1916] 2 Ch. 325.

Comment: The chairman may disqualify himself by improperly adjourning the meeting,[11] vacating the chair or refusing to continue the meeting[12] or to appoint scrutineers after being requested to do so.[13] If the chairman does not act judicially, the court may intervene and correct the wrong.[14]

66. Chairman to continue

Subject to his being disqualified or properly removed, the chairman of the meeting, however selected, shall continue presiding throughout the meeting and all adjournments thereof.[15]

Comment: The chairman, once he is properly in the chair, is not obligated to retire from the chair in favour of a person having a greater right to preside.[16]

67. Duties of chairman

It is the duty of the chairman to enforce the rules of order.[17] The chairman must:

(1) assure that the meeting is duly constituted (Rule 91);

(2) provide reasonable accommodation (Rule 9);

---

[11] *National Dwellings Society v. Sykes*, [1894] 3 Ch. 159. Where the chairman refused to entertain a motion that he vacate the chair, and the majority passed a motion appointing another chairman and turned their chairs around facing the new chairman, it was held to be a validly continued meeting (*Cole v. McCormick*, February 14, 1929, *per* Orde, J., in Weekly Court (unreported)). "Where the chairman frustrates the business of a meeting by wilfully and without good reason preventing that business from being considered, the meeting may, in view of his gross violation of duty, supersede him as Chairman and go on to transact the business. But if in good faith, the Chairman gives a decision upon a matter of difficulty, such as has arisen in connection with the notice in this case, I am not prepared to hold that his decision can be ignored and overturned there and then. In my opinion in such a case, his decision must stand until it is set aside by the Court, or by a general meeting properly convened for that purpose" (*Melville v. Graham-Yooll*, [1936] Scots Law Times 54).

[12] *Van Alstyne v. Rankin*, [1952] Que. S.C. 12. See Rule 20.

[13] By refusing under special circumstances to appoint scrutineers the chairman was held to have abandoned any idea of exercising a proper discretion (*Gray v. Yellowknife Gold Mines, supra*).

[14] *Johnson v. Hall*, 10 D.L.R. (2d) 243, 23 W.W.R. 228 (B.C.S.C.).

[15] Since an adjourned meeting must be regarded as a continuation of the annual meeting, the chairman who presided at the annual meeting is entitled to preside at the adjourned meeting (*Dominion Royalty Corp. v. Holborn* (1932), 41 O.W.N. 288).

[16] He should refuse to retire from the chair if requested (*Freemont Canning Co. & Johnson v. Wall & Fine Foods of Canada Ltd.*, [1940] 4 D.L.R. 86).

[17] "Public meetings must be regulated somehow; and where a number of persons assemble and put a man in the chair, they devolve upon him by agreement the conduct of that body. They attorn to him, as it were, and give him the whole power of regulating themselves individually. The chairman collects his authority from the meeting." (*Per* Jervis, C.J., in *Taylor v. Nesfield* (1855), unreported, quoted in *Wills on Parish Vestries*, p. 29n.)

(3) admit all persons entitled to attend (Rule 7);

(4) preserve order (Rule 68);

(5) appoint scrutineers if requested (Rule 78) and instruct them in their duties;

(6) ascertain the sense of the meeting[18] by a vote on all questions properly brought before the meeting (Rule 151).

68. Preserve order

The chairman must enforce the designated rules of order. He must also preserve and maintain order[19] and do all things necessary for the proper conduct of the meeting.[20]

> *Comment:* The chairman has the right to eject an unruly shareholder.[21] He may order his removal but no undue or unnecessary violence may be used.[22]

69. Act fairly

The chairman must act fairly,[23] in good faith, and without malice. He may be removed by the meeting[24] if he refuses to put proper questions to the meeting.

[18] *Re LeMay Ltd.* (1924), 26 O.W.N. 443; *Henderson v. Bank of Australasia* (1890) 45 Ch. D. 330 (C.A.).

[19] *Re Indian Zoedone Co.* (1884), 26 Ch. D. 70; *Gray v. Yellowknife Gold Mines Ltd.,* [1946] O.W.N. 938; *National Dwellings Society v. Sykes,* [1894] 3 Ch. 159; *Lucas v. Mason* (1875), L.R. 10 Exch. 251.

[20] "It is on the chairman that it devolves both to preserve order in the meeting and to regulate the proceedings so as to give all persons entitled a reasonable opportunity of voting. He is to do the acts necessary for these purposes on his own responsibility, and is subject to being called upon to answer for his conduct if he has done anything improperly" (*R. v. D'Oyly* (1840), 12 Ad. & E. 139, 113 E.R. 763).

[21] *Gray v. Allison* (1909), 25 T.L.R. 531.

[22] *Doyle v. Falconer* (1866) L.R.I.P.C. 340; *Hawkins v. Muff* (1911) 2 Glen's L.G. Cases 151.

[23] "A chairman of a meeting has clearly defined rights and obligations and it does not lie within his power to refuse to carry out his duties because there is submitted to him a motion which is personally distasteful to him". (*Van Alstyne v. Rankin,* [1952] Que. S.C. 12.) See also *Spurr v. Albert* 15 N.B.R. 260, *Freemont Canning Co. & Johnson v. Wall & Fine Foods Ltd.,* [1940] 4 D.L.R. 86, aff'd [1941] 3 D.L.R. 96.

"A presiding officer cannot arbitrarily defeat the will of the majority by refusing to entertain or put motions, by wrongfully declaring the result of a vote, or by refusing to permit the expression by the majority of its will. He is the representative of the body over which he presides. His will is not binding on it, but its will, legally expressed by a majority of its members, is binding." *American Aberdeen-Angus Breeders Ass'n v. Fullerton* 325 Ill. 323, 156 N.E. 314 (1927).

[24] *Van Alstyne v. Rankin & St. Lawrence Corp. Ltd.* [1952] Que. S.C. 12.

Comment: The chairman is not liable in tort if he acts in good faith.[25] His act is similar to a judicial act and he is entitled, if he acts in good faith and without malice, to be protected from liability.[26] He himself may be removed if he persists in clogging the proceedings.[27]

70. Appeals from the chairman

Rulings of the chairman relating to procedural matters arising out of rules of order[28] may be appealed to the meeting. By a majority vote of those present and voting a ruling of the chairman may be reversed or varied.

Comment: Decisions relating to proxies, ballots or results of polls are not appealable to the meeting. If a voter believes that a decision of the chairman or of the meeting is oppressive or unfair he may apply to the courts for an order to rectify the matter.

71. Right to vote

The chairman, while in the chair, is not disqualified from voting. He has no casting vote[29] except where one is specifically granted by statute[30] or the constitution. If the chairman is given a casting vote, he may cast it only if there is an equality of votes.

Comment: The chairman may give a contingent casting vote to become effective if it should appear, when the count is concluded, that there is an equality of valid votes.[31] He cannot use his casting vote as a means of giving himself control of the company.[32]

---

25 *R. v. D'Oyly* (1840), 12 **Ad.** & E. 139, 113 E.R. 763.

26 *Bluechel and Smith v. Prefabricated Buildings Ltd. and Thomas*, [1945] 2 D.L.R. 725. Malice is essential to such an action (*Tozer v. Child and Howard* (1857), 7 El. & Bl. 377, 119 E.R. 1286, following *Cullen v. Morris* (1819), 2 Stark 577, 171 E.R. 741).

27 *Gray v. Yellowknife* [1946] O.W.N. 938.

28 Rule 5.

29 *Re Fireproof Doors, Ltd.*, [1916] 2 Ch. 142; *Bland v. Buchanan*, [1901] 2 K.B. 75; *Nell v. Longbottom*, [1894] 1 Q.B. 767; *Re National Drive-in Theatres Ltd. and Companies Act* (B.C.), [1954] 2 D.L.R. 55.

30 See table inside back cover.

31 *Bland v. Buchanan*, [1901] 2 K.B. 75.

32 *Re Bondi Better Bananas Ltd. and Vallario and Bondi*, [1951] O.R. 410; reversed on other grounds, [1951] O.R. 845 (C.A.); *Re Citizens Coal & Forwarding Co. Ltd.*, [1927] 4 D.L.R. 275.

72. Right to propose or second

The chairman cannot propose or second a motion unless there are only one or two other persons present who are qualified to vote. This rule is based on the expediency of getting on with the business of the meeting.[33]

> *Comment:* If there are more than two other persons present who are qualified to vote and he wishes to propose or second a motion he may retire from the chair.

SECRETARY

73. Appointment

The secretary of the company acts as secretary of the meeting unless, prior to the meeting, some other person has been appointed by the board of directors to act as secretary of the meeting. If there is no duly appointed secretary present and willing to act when the meeting is called to order, the meeting may appoint any person to act as secretary. Such person need not be one qualified to vote.

74. Powers of secretary

The secretary has only those powers specifically given to him by the constitution, the board or the meeting.

> *Comment:* The secretary has no inherent authority to call meetings without a resolution of the board, but such an act may be subsequently ratified by the board.

75. Duties of secretary of meetings of the board

To prepare for meetings of the board, the secretary shall:

1. Assemble agenda material, including all correspondence, agreements, reports and data which may be necessary for the assistance of the directors in considering the matters to be discussed at the next meeting of the board.

2. Prepare notice of meeting in accordance with the bylaws and articles, and have the company's solicitor check notice and prepare draft motions (resolutions) arising out of the material.

3. Fix a date for the meeting which would be most convenient for the majority of directors.

4. Prepare agenda for the meeting. It is sometimes advisable to send a copy of the agenda to the directors in advance so that they may have an indication of the matters to be discussed.

---

[33] See also Rule 122.

5. Arrange for the meeting room, seating accommodation, etc.

6. Attend meeting and take notes of proceedings.

7. Draft minutes of the meeting and have company's solicitor check them.

76. Duties of secretary for annual meetings of shareholders

To prepare for annual meetings the secretary shall:

1. Arrange for the financial statements to be completed and audited.

2. Arrange for annual report. (It ought to contain a letter from the president or the board of directors.)

3. Have the company's solicitor prepare a notice of meeting, proxy form and information circular. (If the company's shares are listed on a stock exchange or under the jurisdiction of a securities commission, their regulations must be complied with.)

4. Arrange for tentative date of meeting and meeting room.

5. Arrange for meeting of the board of directors (Rule 75) to approve the financial statements and the annual report, authorize the calling of the annual meeting, and approve the notice, proxy form and information circular.

6. Arrange for printing of all material to be mailed.

7. Make list of shareholders or arrange for transfer agent to bring share registers and transfer registers to the meeting (or, if a record date has been fixed, a list of shareholders as of the record date).

8. Arrange for mailing to all shareholders of record on or before the record date (check bylaws for record date). Copies of all material should be sent to every appropriate securities commission, stock exchange, and to the company's auditors. If desired, copies may be sent to the press.

9. A copy of all material should be sent to each new shareholder whose name appears on the register after the original mailing.

10. Arrange for publication of the notice of meeting in the press, if required under the articles or bylaws.

11. Arrange for ballots to be printed if opposition is expected.

12. Tabulate proxies as they are received. If there is more than one class of stock they should be sorted. Enter on the proxy form (in different coloured ink) the number of votes which may be voted. Each signature should be compared with the name on the register, and if it does not conform, it should be set to one side for the decision of the chairman.

13. Arrange for the share registers, or a list of shareholders as of the record date, to be at the meeting.

14. Prepare ballots for every motion or election which may be controversial.

15. Prepare scrutineers' reports on attendance and on each ballot which will be taken.

16. Prepare agenda and motions and have the company's solicitor check them (or have the company's solicitor prepare them).

17. Invite the auditor and, if indicated, the company's engineers, managers, the press, etc.

18. Arrange for the physical accommodation, head table, chairs, scrutineers' table, etc.

19. As each shareholder enters the meeting room record his name and holdings. If scrutineers have been appointed they will do this.

20. Arrange with persons entitled to vote to act as "movers" and "seconders" of routine motions.

21. Arrange the head table with the company's minute books, copies of agenda, a supply of annual reports and any other material which may be pertinent to the meeting. (A supply of blank paper should always be handy in case a poll is unexpectedly demanded.)

22. Check presence of scrutineers, share register (list of shareholders).

23. Attend meeting and take notes of proceedings. Where the meeting is likely to be controversial, it is advisable to have a shorthand stenographer (preferably a court reporter) to take verbatim notes of the proceedings.

24. Draft minutes and submit to company's solicitor for approval.

25. Have the chairman sign the minutes (Rule 182).

77. Duties of secretary for special meetings of shareholders

To prepare for special meetings, the secretary shall:

1. Make certain that the company's solicitor has cleared with the appropriate securities commissions and stock exchanges all special bylaws and special resolutions passed by the board and intended to be confirmed by the shareholders.

2. Have the company's solicitor prepare a notice of meeting, proxy form and information circular.

3. Prepare a letter to the shareholders from the board or the president explaining the purposes of the meeting.

4. Have a meeting of the board of directors to approve the letter, the notice of meeting, proxy form and information circular.

5. Follow the procedure in Rule 76, items 4 to 25.

SCRUTINEERS

78. Appointment of scrutineers

The chairman may at any time, and shall, at the request of the shareholders, appoint one or more scrutineers to assist him in taking the attendance and counting proxies and ballots. Scrutineers need not be entitled to vote at the meeting.

> *Comment:* The appointment of scrutineers is not mandatory[34] except when demanded by the shareholders.[35] The appointment may be made at any time before or during the meeting. Scrutineers should preferably be independent parties.[36]

---

[34] *Wandsworth & Putney Gas Light & Coke Co. v. Wright* (1870), 22 L.T. 404.

[35] At the request of a shareholder the chairman shall appoint scrutineers. The refusal to appoint scrutineers after the request of a shareholder is improper (*Gray v. Yellowknife Gold Mines Ltd.*, [1946] O.W.N. 938).

[36] Shareholders are not incapable of being scrutineers but it would certainly be better that persons outside the company be chosen (*Watt v. Commonwealth Petroleum Ltd.*, [1938] 4 D.L.R. 701). Directors of a company also being candidates for re-election cannot be scrutineers because of conflict of interest and duty (*Dickson v. McMurray* (1881), 28 Gr. 533).

79. Duties of scrutineers

The scrutineers shall, at the request of the chairman and as expeditiously as possible:

(1) report in detail on the attendance at the meeting;

(2) collect, examine and tabulate proxies;

(3) report in detail to the chairman;

(4) collect, examine and tabulate ballots;

(5) report in detail and return all proxies and ballots to the chairman.

The scrutineers shall check the persons present and the proxies filed against the shareholders' register or list of shareholders, tabulate the proxies noting the appointees, any special instructions or limitations noted thereon. In case of a poll, they shall check for defective ballots, tabulate the votes cast for and against each motion (Form 24) or candidate (Form 26). Scrutineers have no right to retain proxies or ballots, but must return them to the chairman with their report without delay. The chairman is not obligated to accept the report of the scrutineers.[37]

> *Comment:* The scrutineers' duties are ministerial not judicial.[38] They shall not question a proxy which on its face appears to be genuine and valid. They cannot determine any disputed proxies but should report them without delay to the chairman for his decision. The chairman will examine and consider the defective and disputed ballots and proxies and rule on them (Rules 166 and 191).[39]

80. Discharge of scrutineers

Scrutineers having completed their report are automatically discharged. Scrutineers may be discharged or replaced by the shareholders at any time.[40] Scrutineers appointed by the chairman may be discharged or replaced by the chairman at any time.

QUORUM

81. Quorum—definition

A quorum is the minimum number of persons qualified to vote whose presence at a meeting is requisite in order that business

---

37 *Montreal Trust Co. v. Oxford Pipe Line Co.,* [1942] 2 D.L.R. 703; aff'd [1942] 3 D.L.R. 619.

38 *Dickson v. McMurray, supra.*

39 *Montreal Trust Co. v. Oxford Pipe Line Co., supra.*

40 See footnote 35, *supra.*

may be validly transacted. In the absence of a quorum, no business can be conducted[41] except to adjourn. The number constituting the quorum is determined by the statute or the constitution of the company.

> *Comment:* Where a quorum is fixed by statute, acts performed in the absence of a quorum are invalid.[42] If permitted by the constitution, a board, lacking a quorum, may fill vacancies.

82. Quorum—shareholders meeting

Unless fixed by the statute[43] or the constitution, two shareholders are sufficient to constitute a quorum.[44] The court has no power to direct that one shareholder present in person or by proxy shall be deemed to constitute a meeting.[45]

> *Comment:* Under the common law a quorum consists of a majority of the members.

83. Quorum count

The presence of a quorum may be questioned and a quorum count demanded at any time. For this purpose the discussion may be interrupted, but not while a speaker has the floor. The chairman may then count the attendance. This motion does not require seconding, is not amendable or debatable and does not require a vote. It is in the nature of a demand.

> *Comment:* If the chairman is satisfied that a quorum is present he rejects the demand. If a count is proceeded with and it shows that a quorum is not present, the meeting must be adjourned (Rule 174).

> *Motion:* "Mr. Chairman, is a quorum present?" *or* "Mr. Chairman, I suggest the absence of a quorum."

---

41 *Armstrong v. McGibbon* (1906), 15 Que. K.B. 345; *Lumbers v. Fretz* (1928) 63 O.L.R. 190.

42 *D'Arcy v. Tamar* (1867) L.R. 2 Ex. 159.

43 See table inside back cover.

44 *Re Cowichan Leader Ltd.* (1963) 42 D.L.R. (2d) 111.

45 *Morrill v. Little Falls Mfg. Co.* 53 Minn. 371 (1893), quoted by Hope, J., in *Montreal Trust Co. v. Oxford Pipe Line Co.,* [1942] 2 D.L.R. 703; aff'd [1942] 3 D.L.R. 619; *R. v. Bellringer* (1792) 4 T.R. 810, 100 E.R. 1315.

84. Counting proxyholder in quorum

A proxyholder who is also a shareholder is counted as only one person in a quorum count regardless of how many shareholders he represents, but all the shares he represents may be included in any quorum requirement for a specific number of shares.[46] A proxyholder who is not a shareholder is counted as a shareholder present.[47]

> *Comment:* One shareholder cannot constitute a quorum even if he represents another proxy[46] unless together they constitute all the shareholders (see Rule 86).

85. Disqualified persons

Persons disqualified from voting by reason of being interested in the question cannot be counted in determining whether a quorum is present.[48]

> *Comment:* If a director of the company is a shareholder of the contracting company, he is an interested party and must refrain from voting[49] at a meeting of the board.

86. Quorum lacking

In the absence of a quorum, no business can be conducted[50] except to adjourn to a fixed time and place (Rule 174).

> *Comment:* Where the statute requires a meeting to be held, the attendance of one shareholder only[51] even with proxies in his favour, will not constitute a meeting.[52] But one holder of all the issued shares of a class may constitute a meeting.[53] For board meetings lacking a quorum see Rule 81.

---

[46] *Sharp v. Dawes* (1876), 2 Q.B.D. 26; *Re Sanitary Carbon Co.*, [1877] W.N. 223.

[47] *Ernest v. Loma Gold Mines Ltd.* [1897] 1 Ch. 1.

[48] *Garvie v. Axmith* (1961), 31 D.L.R. (2d) 65; *Ferguson v. Wallbridge*, [1935] 3 D.L.R. 66; *Re North Eastern Ins. Co. Ltd.*, [1919] 1 Ch. 198; *Doig v. Mathews* (1915), 25 D.L.R. 732; *Re D. & S. Drug Co.* (1916), 10 W.W.R. 612, rev'd 31 D.L.R. 643; *Yuill v. Greymouth Point Elizabeth Rly. & Coal Co. Ltd.*, [1904] 1 Ch. 32; *Doig v. Port Edward Townsite Co. Ltd.* (1916), 22 B.C.R. 418; *Doig v. Mathews, supra.*

[49] *Garvie v. Axmith, supra; Transvaal Lands Co. v. New Belgium (Transvaal) Land & Development Co.*, [1914] 2 Ch. 488; *Gray v. Yellowknife Gold Mines Ltd. and Bear Exploration & Radium Ltd.*, [1948] 1 D.L.R. 473.

[50] *Armstrong v. McGibbon* (1906), 15 Que. K.B. 345; *Re Keyes and Hope Trading Syndicate* [1949] O.W.N. 307.

[51] *Re Primary Distributors Ltd.*, [1954] 2 D.L.R. 438; *Re Cowichan Leader Ltd.* (1963) 42 D.L.R. (2d) 111; *Sharp v. Dawes, supra; East v. Bennett Bros. Ltd.*, [1911] 1 Ch. 163; *Re Keyes*, [1949] 3 D.L.R. 299; *Re Sanitary Carbon Co., supra.*

[52] *Re Keyes, supra; Re Sanitary Carbon Co., supra*

[53] *East v. Bennett Bros. Ltd., supra; Re Woodward*, [1940] O.R. 387.

87. Quorum disappearing

A meeting cannot continue once a quorum disappears, even though the meeting was validly opened with a quorum present.[54] Unless the constitution otherwise provides, the meeting must be adjourned or it automatically lapses. Business transacted at a meeting lacking a quorum is invalid.[55] If a quorum is present at the opening of a meeting and no quorum count is taken or demanded, it is presumed that a quorum continued to be present throughout the meeting.[56]

> *Comment:* If a meeting is adjourned by reason of the lack of a quorum, a new notice is required.

88. Withdrawing shareholder bound

A shareholder who attends a meeting and withdraws is bound by the lawful acts of those who remain and carry on the meeting, provided that the quorum requirements are satisfied.

> *Comment:* Shareholders who attend a meeting and then without cause voluntarily withdraw are in no better position than those who voluntarily absent themselves in the first instance,[57] and they are not in a position to complain about the acts of those who remain and perform their duties in a regular and lawful manner.[58]

AGENDA

89. Agenda

The order of business to be conducted by the meeting is prepared by the secretary prior to the meeting. The purpose of the meeting is established by either the requirements of the governing statute or the exigency of the business of the company.

---

54 *Lumbers v. Fretz,* [1928] 4 D.L.R. 269, aff'd [1929] 1 D.L.R. 51; *Henderson v. Louttit & Co. Ltd.* (1894), 31 Sc. L.R. 555.

55 *Sovereen Mitt, Glove, and Robe Co. v. Whitside* (1906), 12 O.L.R. 638; *Foster v. Foster,* [1916] 1 Ch. 532; *Armstrong v. McGibbon* (1906), 15 Que. K.B. 345; *Lubin v. Draeger* (1918), 144 L. T. Jo. 274; *Re Alma Spinning Co.* (1880), 16 Ch. D. 681.

56 *United States v. Bryan,* 339 U.S. 323 (1950).

57 *Commonwealth v. Vandegrift,* 232 Pa. St. 53 (1911).

58 *Famous Players Canadian Corp. Ltd. v. Hamilton United Theatres Ltd.,* [1944] 3 D.L.R. 134.

OPENING OF MEETING
90. Time

If the chairman is present, the meeting may be opened at the time specified in the notice or within a period of fifteen minutes thereof.

> *Comment:* The meeting must not be opened prior to the time specified[59] nor precipitately on the hour if more voters are expected.[60] If the chairman is not present, see Rule 63.

91. Opening the meeting

When the chairman is satisfied that he is properly in the chair, he calls the meeting to order. When he is satisfied that proper notice has been given and a quorum is present, he declares the meeting duly constituted for the transaction of business.

The usual procedure for opening a meeting is as follows:

1. *Chairman:* "The meeting will please come to order."

2. He declares his authority for being in the chair.

3. He states the authority of the secretary to act as secretary. He may appoint a secretary prior to the meeting or ask the meeting to appoint one. (See Rule 103.)

4. He satisfies himself that the notice was signed by the proper authority and was mailed to every person entitled to vote at the meeting.

5. He may request the secretary to read the notice and proof of service of notice[61] or ask the meeting whether it desires them to be read.

6. He may instruct the secretary to annex the notice and proof of service to the minutes of the meeting.

7. He satisfies himself that a quorum is present (Rules 81, 86). If an exact count of the attendance has not been completed, but it appears to him that a quorum is present, the chairman may carry on with the meeting or he may wait for an actual count from the secretary or the scrutineers.

8. He declares the meeting duly constituted for the transaction of business.

---

59 *Fuller v. Bruce*, [1935] 3 D.L.R. 256; aff'd [1936] S.C.R. 124.
60 *Armstrong v. McGibbon* (1906), 15 Que. K.B. 345; aff'g 29 Que. S.C. 289.
61 Rule 54.

Chairman: "I declare that this meeting is duly constituted for the transaction of business."

9. The minutes of the previous meeting need not be but may be verified by the shareholders by resolution (Rule 185). If copies of the minutes have been previously distributed to the shareholders, a shareholder may move that the minutes be taken as read, in which case the reading may be dispensed with. If not the minutes may be read by the secretary. Dealing with the minutes of the previous meeting is not necessary but is desirable.

Motion: "I move that the minutes of the meeting of shareholders held . . . be hereby taken as read (and verified)."

10. The chairman now asks whether there are any errors or omissions in the minutes (Rule 186). Anyone who was present at the meeting, the minutes of which are under discussion, may point out any errors or omissions, and move that the minutes be verified (and adopted) with or without correction, deletions or additions.

Chairman: "You have heard the minutes. Are there any errors or omissions? Will someone move that the minutes be verified and adopted?"

11. The meeting is now open for business.

ENFORCING CORRECT PROCEDURE

92. Point of order

A point of order demand enables a voter: (1) to insist on strict compliance with the rules of order; and (2) to draw attention to a violation of the rules of order. For this purpose, the speaker (Rule 149) and the discussion may be interrupted (Rule 150). All proceedings stop until the point of order has been decided. Although not a motion, it takes precedence over all motions except closing motions (Rule 173) and quorum count (Rule 83) and must be decided immediately. It can have no motion applied to it except a motion to withdraw (Rule 128). If the point deals with procedure, it must be raised immediately. If it deals with a violation of the law or the bylaws, it may be raised at any time. The chairman's ruling is final unless overruled by the court (Rules 70 and 155). It does not require seconding, is not amendable or debatable and does not require a vote.

Comment: It is the duty of the chairman to enforce the rules of order (Rule 67) and of the voters present to insist upon the enforcement of the rules of order (Rule 1). Upon the raising of a point of order, discussion ceases. If the chairman or a voter is speaking, he stops and resumes his seat. The chairman asks the interrupter to state his point of order briefly. No speech or debate or amendment is permissible, but a brief explanation is in order. He may consult a manual of rules of order or request the sense of the meeting. If the point is accepted, the chairman corrects the situation. If the point is not accepted, the chairman so declares and the meeting resumes.

Motion: "Mr. Chairman, point of order. My point of order is that . . ."

93. Parliamentary inquiry

A demand for parliamentary inquiry enables a voter to ask the chairman or the speaker questions regarding the procedure being or to be followed, or the result of such procedure. For this purpose, the speaker may be interrupted. All proceedings stop until the parliamentary inquiry has been dealt with. Although not a motion, it takes precedence over all motions except closing motions (Rule 173) and quorum count demand (Rule 83) and must be dealt with immediately. It does not require seconding, is not amendable or debatable and does not require a vote.

Comment: Every voter has the right to know the proper parliamentary procedure and it is the duty of the chairman to acquaint himself with the rules of order. The questions asked must be *bona fide* and not argumentative or challenging.

Motion: "Mr. Chairman, I rise to a parliamentary inquiry. Is it necessary to . . .?"

or "Mr. Chairman, does this motion require a two-thirds majority?"

or "Mr. Chairman, may I ask a question on parliamentary procedure?"

94. Point of information

A point of information demand is to enable a voter to have answered basic questions which are necessary to the understanding of the motion on the floor. For this purpose the speaker may be interrupted. All proceedings stop until the point of information has been dealt with. Although not a motion, it takes precedence over all motions except closing motions (Rule 173) and quorum count (Rule 83) and must be dealt with immediately. It does not require seconding, is not amendable or debatable and does not require a vote.

> *Comment:* Every voter has the right to have the motion read to him, to have his questions answered regarding the result of the vote on the motion, and technical and statistical data relative thereto, but the question must be *bona fide* and not argumentative or challenging.

> *Motion:* "Mr. Chairman, I rise to a point of information", *or* "Mr. Chairman, may I ask a question?", *or* "Mr. Chairman, may I ask the speaker a question?" *or* "Mr. Chairman, will you please read the motion on the floor?"

95. Question of privilege

Each person who has the right to attend the meeting may raise a question of privilege if his personal comfort, right or convenience at the meeting is wanting,[62] or if he cannot hear or be heard or has been subjected to insult or abuse. On a question of privilege, the speaker and the discussion may be interrupted. All proceedings stop until the matter has been dealt with. Although not a motion, it takes precedence over all motions except closing motions and must be dealt with immediately. It does not require seconding, is not amendable or debatable and does not require a vote.

> *Comment:* All persons having the right to vote are entitled to hear all the proceedings and to be heard. It is the duty of the chairman to insure that they do.[63] In response to a question of privilege the chairman should correct the situation complained of. If the question of privilege was raised with respect to the language of a previous speaker he may demand a retraction, apology or change of attitude.

> *Motion:* "Mr. Chairman, a question of privilege: The light is so poor I cannot read the report" *or* "Mr. Chairman, a question of privilege: Would you mind speaking a little louder, we at the rear cannot hear you" *or* "Mr. Chairman, a question of privilege: The public address system is not working" *or* "Mr. Chairman, a question of privilege: Mr. . . . says, etc."

---

62 Rule 9.
63 Rule 8.

ELECTIONS AND APPOINTMENTS

ELECTIONS

96. Elections

An election is the act of choosing freely from a number of persons. The directors are elected[1] by the shareholders. The president, the chairman of the board and other officers are elected or appointed[2] by the board of directors in accordance with the statute or the constitution. Vacancies on the board are filled by appointment. The appointment may be made by the board of directors if a quorum remains in office, or by the shareholders. Where cumulative voting for the election of directors is provided for, each shareholder is entitled to cast a number of votes equal to the number of votes attached to the shares held by him multiplied by the number of directors to be elected.

> Comment: Upon the due election of directors, whether at an annual or special meeting called for that purpose, the term of office of the former directors automatically expires.[3] Failure to mail financial statements to the shareholders in accordance with the statute does not necessarily invalidate an election of directors at an annual meeting.[4]

---

[1] See the statute or the bylaws as to whether the vacancy is to be filled by election or appointment.

[2] "The election of a corporation officer is only a method of appointment and confers no greater or different right than if he were appointed and vice versa" (Van Alstyne v. Rankin, [1952] Que. S.C. 12).

[3] Gold-Rex Kirkland Mines Ltd. v. Morrow, [1944] 4 D.L.R. 779; McEachren (W.N.) & Sons, Ltd.; Re McGibbon v. Imperial Trust Co., [1933] 2 D.L.R. 558.

[4] Watt v. Commonwealth Petroleum Ltd., [1938] 4 D.L.R. 701 (Alta. C.A.).

97. Nominations

A nomination is the proposing of a candidate for election to an office to be filled. Every person entitled to vote may nominate one or more candidates. If the election is for a board of directors, he need not nominate a full board. He need not vote for a full board. A nomination does not require seconding and is not debatable or amendable. The person nominated may decline the nomination at any time and his name is thereupon withdrawn.

Comment: There is no such thing as a "slate of directors".

Procedure: The chairman declares the meeting open for the election of whatever offices are to be filled: "The meeting is open for the election of directors. Five are required. Anyone may nominate any number of candidates up to five".

Motion: "I nominate A, B, C, D, and E as directors of the company",
or "I nominate F as one of the directors".

98. Motion to close nominations

Nominations may be closed by the chairman after a reasonable time has elapsed or by resolution of the voters. A speaker may not be interrupted for this motion. A motion to close nominations requires seconding and is not debatable.

Chairman: "Are there any more nominations?"

Motion: "I move the nominations be closed."

Chairman: "Before consideration of this motion, are there any more nominations?"

99. Procedure if required number nominated

If only the number of candidates required to fill the office or offices is nominated and nominations are properly closed,[5] the chairman declares the persons nominated to be elected to the offices by acclamation, or asks for a motion to declare the person or persons nominated elected by acclamation. A motion to declare the nominees elected dispenses with a formal election when a ballot is not specifically required by the constitution. It requires seconding and is not amendable or debatable. A majority vote is required. If the constitution requires elections to be by ballot, the chairman distributes ballots and holds an election by ballot, or he

---

[5] Rule 98.

may call for a motion directing the secretary to cast a single ballot on behalf of the persons entitled to vote for the election of those nominated. This motion requires seconding and is not debatable or amendable. A majority vote is required.

> *Motion:* "Resolved that the secretary of the meeting is hereby directed to cast a ballot for the election of . . . . as . . . ."
>
> *Form:* "On behalf of all the shareholders I hereby cast a ballot for the election of . . . . , (Signed) *Secretary.*"
>
> *Comment:* See procedure set out in Rule 100, *infra.*

100. Procedure if more than the required number nominated

If more than the required number are nominated, a poll is required[6] and it shall be taken at once. Ballots are distributed, collected, counted and the result declared.

The procedure may be as follows:

1. A ballot is handed to every person entitled to vote. The ballot may be either a blank paper or a paper containing the names of the persons nominated.

2. The chairman instructs those entitled to vote as to the manner of voting: if it is a blank ballot, to write the names of the candidates of their choice on the paper, or, if it is a printed ballot, to mark an "X" opposite the candidates of their choice.

3. Those entitled to vote are instructed to write their names at the foot of the ballot; and, if voting by proxy, to add the words "for self and those who appointed me their proxy" or "on behalf of . . ." giving name(s) of shareholder(s), or words to that effect.

4. The chairman collects the ballots, examines them, decides their validity and counts the votes cast. The chairman may appoint scrutineers to assist him in collecting, examining and counting the votes, but only the chairman may rule on the validity of the ballots (Rules 167, 168).

5. The chairman announces the result (Rule 155).

101. Declaration as to election

On the completion of the election, whether by acclamation, single ballot or poll, the chairman declares the successful candidates duly elected to office.

---

6 Rule 163.

APPOINTMENTS

102. Motion to appoint

A motion to appoint is the act of naming a person or persons to an office or offices. There is no choice or selection indicated. Only the number of candidates required to fill the vacancies may be named in a motion to appoint and each must be qualified to hold the office. This motion requires seconding and is not amendable or debatable.

> *Comment:* Auditors, vice-presidents, secretaries, and assistant secretaries, treasurers and assistant treasurers, vacancies in the board and transfer agencies, are appointed unless the constitution provides otherwise.[7]

103. Procedure for appointments

A motion to appoint follows the same procedure as any other motion:[8]

1. The chairman calls for a motion to fill the vacant office.

2. He receives a motion to appoint a qualified person to the office.

> *Chairman:* "May I have a motion to appoint a secretary of the meeting?"
>
> *A voter:* "I move that Mr. A. be appointed secretary of the meeting."

3. The chairman deals with the motion in the required manner. Anyone desiring the appointment of a different person may vote against the motion and if the motion is defeated, he may move for the appointment of the candidate of his choice.

4. If the motion to appoint is carried, the chairman declares the person named appointed to that office.[9] If the motion to appoint is defeated, the chairman requests another motion to appoint, naming another person and so on until a motion to appoint is carried.

---

[7] After an annual meeting, officers must be appointed, as the tenure of office of officers expires upon the election of a new board of directors (*Ghimpelman v. Bercovici,* [1957] S.C.R. 128).

[8] Rules 104 and subsequent.

[9] Rule 101.

MOTIONS AND RESOLUTIONS

Note: for the characteristics of all motions and their order of precedence, see the Table on the inside front cover.

RESOLUTIONS

104. Resolutions and motions

A motion is a proposal to do something, to order something to be done or to express an opinion about something[1] The subject matter of a motion is called "the question". A motion, when duly passed, becomes a resolution, which is a corporate resolve. Every corporate act requires a resolution. Acts of officers and directors are authorized or approved by resolution either before or after they are done. Adoption of reports is done by resolution.

Comment: A resolution applies to a single act of the corporation in contrast to a bylaw, which is a permanent continuing rule of the corporation applied to all future occasions.

---

[1] A bylaw may be enacted in the form of a resolution where the object to be accomplished is properly the subject of a bylaw. (*Mackenzie v. Maple Mountain Mining* (1910) 20 O.L.R. 615.)

In the absence of statutory authority[2] a resolution signed by all the shareholders but not passed at a meeting is not valid.

105. Types of resolutions

There are three types of resolutions, each requiring a different majority:

— ordinary resolutions (Rule 106);

— special resolutions (Rule 107);

— extraordinary resolutions (Rule 108).

106. Resolutions (ordinary)

Resolutions are decisions made by a body of persons entitled to vote. It applies to a single act of the body.[3] An ordinary resolution is a motion passed by a simple majority (over 50 per cent) which is sufficient for most purposes.[4] For some purposes, the statute or the constitution requires that the motion be passed by a greater majority.[5]

107. Special resolutions

The statute[4] or the constitution may require some corporate acts to be done by special resolution, that is, one requiring at least two-thirds of the votes cast.

> *Comment:* In Ontario, a special resolution is a resolution passed by at least two-thirds of the votes cast at a special meeting of the shareholders of the corporation duly called for that purpose.

108. Extraordinary resolutions

The statute or the constitution may require some corporate acts to be done by extraordinary resolution, that is, one requiring more than two-thirds of the votes cast.

MOTIONS GENERALLY

109. Kinds of motions

There are four kinds of motions:

— main motions (Rule 110) which originate business;

---

2 *Bartlett v. Bartlett Mines Ltd.* (1911) 24 O.L.R. 419 (C.A.); *Newman & Co., Re*, [1895] 1 Ch. 674 (C.A.). However some statutes (e.g. Ontario) permit this procedure.

3 *Mackenzie v. Maple Mountain Mining Co.* (1910) 20 O.L.R. 615.

4 See Rule 6.

5 See table inside back cover.

— subsidiary motions (Rule 111) which modify or dispose of the main motions;

— incidental motions (Rule 112) which arise incidentally out of the business being considered;

— closing motions (Rules 113, 173) which close the meeting permanently or temporarily.

110. Main motions

Main motions originate business, direct, authorize, adopt, ratify, approve, confirm or reject actions. A speaker or the discussion may not be interrupted for a main motion. It requires seconding, is amendable and debatable and requires a simple majority unless the statute[5] or the constitution requires otherwise. It has no precedence and applies to no other motion. It can have applied to it subsidiary motions or motions to withdraw or object to consideration.

111. Subsidiary motions

These motions deal with the main motion. The discussion may be interrupted for subsidiary motions but not while a speaker has the floor. They require seconding and take precedence over main motions but not over incidental[6] or closing motions.[7] The following are subsidiary motions:[8]

(1) Vote immediately (Rule 148);

(2) Close discussion (Rule 148);

(3) Adjourn discussion (Rule 144);

(4) Postpone discussion (Rule 144);

(5) Postpone indefinitely (Rule 145);

(6) Refer or refer back (Rule 146);

(7) Amend motion (Rule 133);

(8) Divide a motion (on demand) (Rule 120);

(9) Divide a motion (by motion) (Rule 121).

112. Incidental motions

Incidental motions arise incidentally out of the business under consideration and concern the rights and privileges of the share-

---

5 See table inside back cover.

6 Rule 112.

7 Rules 113, 173—176.

8 See table inside front cover.

holder. They deal with procedure and take precedence over main and subsidiary motions but not over closing motions. The order of incidental motions is based upon the order in which the movers are recognized by the chairman. Incidental motions[8] are motions to:

(1) Count quorum (Rule 83);

(2) Point of order (Rule 92);

(3) Parliamentary inquiry (Rule 93);

(4) Point of information (Rule 94);

(5) Question of privilege (Rule 95);

(6) Withdraw motion (Rule 128);

(7) Object to consideration (Rule 147).

113. Closing motions

Closing motions are motions dealing with the termination or suspension of the meeting. As privileged motions, they have the highest priority.[9]

114. Order of precedence of motions

Each motion has its own order of priority.[10] When a motion is under discussion, a motion of higher priority may be proposed but not a motion of lower priority.

> *Comment:* The order of precedence is based upon the degree of urgency. See index for specific motions and inside front cover for order of priority.

115. Right to move

Every person entitled to vote, other than the chairman of the meeting (unless there are only two or three qualified voters present[11]) has the right to propose motions or amendments that are in order.

> *Comment:* The chairman cannot propose a motion if there are more than three persons present entitled to vote.[11] If he wishes to propose a motion, he should retire from the chair and a new chairman should be elected (Rule 64), or he may ask a voter to move the motion.

---

[8] See table inside front cover.
[9] See Rule 170 and table inside front cover.
[10] See table inside front cover.
[11] See Rule 123.

116. Procedure for proposing a motion

The procedure for a motion is as follows:

1. A person having the right to vote indicates to the chairman his desire for the floor (Rule 141) and when recognized, rises and proposes his motion.

2. If it is a motion which requires seconding (Rule 125) the chairman asks for a seconder. If no seconder is forthcoming the motion is rejected.

3. The chairman considers its relevancy and its form (Rule 140) and, if satisfied that it is in order, calls for discussion on the motion.

4. If there is any confusion about the wording of the motion, or any doubt as to its exact meaning and effect, the chairman may ask the proposer to repeat, explain or clarify it.

5. When discussion has ended (Rule 143) the chairman restates the motion and decides upon the method of voting (Rule 153).

6. The vote is taken (Rules 161 to 166).

7. The chairman declares the result (Rule 155).

117. Demands

A demand is a request made to the chairman to assert a parliamentary right. It requires the immediate attention of the chairman. If the chairman refuses or if the demander is dissatisfied with the result he may restate the demand as a motion.

> *Comment:* See Count Quorum (Rule 83), Point of Order (Rule 92), Parliamentary Inquiry (Rule 93), Point of Information (Rule 94), Question of Privilege (Rule 95), Object to Consideration (Rule 147), Divide a Motion (Rule 120).

CONTENTS OF MOTIONS

118. Contents

All motions and amendments must begin with the word "that" and be:

— relevant;

— in the affirmative;

— within the power and scope of the meeting;

— not argumentative;

— not offensive;

— without unnecessary provisions;

— without objectionable words.

119. Divisibility

Motions are divisible. A motion shall contain only one proposition. When two or more propostions are contained in one motion and each one is so separate and distinct as to be complete in itself if the others are rejected, the chairman may divide them into separate motions and deal with each one separately, or he may divide them into separate paragraphs and deal with each paragraph separately. Division may be made by the chairman on his own volition or on a demand or motion by a voter. The consent of the mover or seconder of the original motion is unnecessary.

120. Demand to divide

A demand to divide a motion is a request for the chairman to divide the motion. Discussion may be interrupted for a demand to divide a motion, but not while a speaker has the floor.

> *Comment:* This is a demand and accordingly does not have the characteristics of a motion. See Rule 121 if the chairman refuses to divide the motion pursuant to a demand.

> *Form:* "I suggest [request *or* demand] that the motion be divided into two separate motions: one: that . . . , and two: that . . ."

121. Motion to divide

A motion to divide a motion must be explicit in setting out the manner of division. The chairman shall accept a motion to divide even if he has rejected a demand to divide.[12] For this purpose, discussion on the main motion may be interrupted but not while a speaker has the floor. A motion to divide requires seconding and is not amendable. A motion to divide may be debated only with respect to the wisdom of making the division and takes precedence over the main motion and a motion to postpone indefinitely. It applies to all main motions and amendments which are divisible and can have no other motion applied to it except a motion to with-

---

[12] See Rule 120.

draw. Voters may propose different divisions and each proposal is dealt with in the order in which each is proposed until one is acceptable to the meeting.

> *Form:* "I move that the motion be divided into two separate motions: one to read as follows: "that etc.," and the other to read as follows: "that etc.".

SECONDING MOTIONS

122. Seconding motions

All closing motions,[13] all subsidiary motions,[14] and a motion to withdraw a motion after the latter has been stated by the chairman[15] and all main motions[16] require seconding. If there is no seconder to the motion, the chairman may refuse to accept the motion or to permit discussion on it. Seconding a motion does not express approval of it but merely indicates an interest in having it discussed and voted on. There is no obligation on the part of the seconder to vote in favour of the motion.

> *Comment:* Under common law, seconding a motion is not essential since the right to move is an individual right.[17] (Seconding of motions is not a requirement in the U.S. Senate). However, if there is no seconder it would appear that no person entitled to vote is willing to put the motion into the discussion stage. To save time the chairman may decline the motion. (See Rule 123 for exceptions.)

123. No seconder

Where there are three or fewer qualified voters present, the chairman may dispense with the requirement for seconding or may himself second a motion.[18]

> *Comment:* This is a rule based upon expediency. The purpose of rules of order is to expedite the business and obtain the sense of the meeting with the minimum of delays. It permits every qualified voter to propose a motion and to have it voted on.

---

13 Rules 113, 173 to 175.

14 Rule 111.

15 Rule 128.

16 Rule 110.

17 *Henderson v. Bank of Australasia* (1890), 45 Ch. D. 330. "There is no law of the land which says that a motion cannot be put without a seconder, and the objection that the amendment was not seconded cannot prevail." (*Re Horbury Bridge Coal, Iron & Waggon Co.* (1879), 11 Ch. D. 109.)

18 See Rule 72.

REVIEWING RESOLUTIONS

124. Rescind resolution

A motion to rescind a resolution, if passed, nullifies the resolution. For this motion, the discussion on the floor may not be interrupted. It requires seconding, is not amenable but is debatable. It applies to all resolutions which have not been acted upon. A motion to rescind cannot be applied to a resolution to rescind. It can have all motions applied to it except those which defer or delay consideration of it. It requires the same majority as did the original motion.[19] If the resolution it proposes to rescind required notice, a vote on a motion to rescind also requires notice and the vote must be taken at a subsequent meeting. A motion to "expunge from the minutes" may be added to the motion to rescind if the passage of the resolution may prove undesirable or embarrassing.

> *Comment:* A resolution cannot be rescinded if it authorizes payment to be made and payment has been made, or if it elected or appointed someone to office and that person was present or has been notified, or if it approved a contract and the other party was present or has been notified.

> *Motion:* "I move that the resolution to . . . passed earlier today be rescinded [and that the same be expunged from the minutes]."

125. Reconsider resolution

A motion to reconsider a resolution may be moved by anyone who voted in favour of it, and, if passed, cancels the vote and the resolution and revives the motion and the discussion on the motion. The discussion on the floor may not be interrupted for a motion to rescind. It requires seconding and is not amenable, but is debatable. It takes precedence as a main motion and can apply to all resolutions which have not been acted upon. It can have all motions applied to it except those which defer or delay consideration of it. It requires the same majority as did the original motion.[20] If the resolution to be reconsidered required notice, so does the vote on the motion to reconsider.

> *Comment:* A resolution cannot be reconsidered if it authorizes payment to be made and payment has been made or if it

[19] Rules 106, 107, 108.
[20] Rules 106, 107, 108.

elected or appointed someone to office and that person was present or was notified, or if it approved a contract and the other party was present or has been notified.

Motion: "I move that the resolution to . . . passed earlier today [*or* on the . . .] be reconsidered."

126. Make resolution unanimous

A motion to make a resolution unanimous, if passed, does not alter the vote on the original motion but superposes an additional result. It may be proposed only by a person who voted against the original motion. The discussion on the floor may not be interrupted for this motion. It requires seconding and is not debatable or amendable.

> *Comment:* This motion is complimentary only and is used to display loyalty by the defeated side to the successful side. Therefore it may be moved only by a person who voted against the motion. A defeated candidate for an office or a shareholder who led an opposition group, as in a proxy contest, may propose this motion as a show of good sportsmanship.

> *Motion:* "I move that the resolution [*or* appointment, *or* election] . . . be made unanimous."

SUPPRESSING MOTIONS

127. Motion out of order

A motion or an amendment must be relevant to the subject, proposed at the proper time, within the power of the meeting, and the scope of the constitution and the governing statute,[21] otherwise the chairman shall declare it out of order. Once a motion is declared out of order it cannot be discussed or voted upon. The same rule applies to an amendment.[22] If the motion is partially irregular, it is rendered wholly irregular and shall be declared out of order.

128. Withdrawal of motion

The mover of a motion (or amendment) may withdraw or modify it before it has been stated by the chairman or seconded. After it has been stated by the chairman or seconded, it can be

---

21 See inside back cover.
22 Rule 133.

withdrawn only with the unanimous consent of the meeting or by
a vote in favour of such withdrawal. A speaker may not be interrupted for the purpose of withdrawing a motion. The motion to
withdraw requires seconding and is not amendable or debatable.
It takes precedence over all motions except closing motions and
can apply to any motion. When it is withdrawn, all subsidiary
motions attached to it collapse.

> *Comment:* The chairman may ask the meeting if it has any
> objection to the withdrawal of the motion. If there are no
> objections (complete acquiescence), permission is granted
> and the motion is withdrawn. If, however, there is even
> one objection, a vote must be taken on the motion to with-
> draw. If the motion to withdraw passes, the mover may
> withdraw the original motion. If the motion is defeated,
> permission is refused and the original motion must be pro-
> ceeded with even against the wishes of the mover.

> *Form: (Before seconding):* "Mr. Chairman, I wish to with-
> draw my motion" *or*

> *(After seconding):* "Mr. Chairman, I ask leave to with-
> draw my motion," *or* "I move that Mr. A. be permitted to
> withdraw his motion" *or*

> *(After being stated):* "Is there any objection to Mr. A.
> withdrawing his motion?"

AMENDMENTS

129. Nature of amendments

Main motions and amendments to main motions may be
amended any number of times, but only one amendment is in
order at one time. It may be amended or altered by an amendment to add, delete, or substitute words or figures. The amendment must be relevant to the motion and may be either compatible
with or hostile to it, but cannot be a simple negation of it. It must
not be of such a nature that the original motion loses its identity.

> *Comment:* If the proposed amendment does not conform with
> this rule, it is ruled out of order.

130. Motions amendable

Main motions (those which originate business) and amendments to main motions are freely amendable. Other motions are
either restrictively amendable or not amendable.

131. Motions restrictively amendable

The following motions are restrictively amendable: to adjourn, to recess and to postpone discussions (as to date, time and place only); and to refer or refer back (as to conditions of reference only).[23]

132. Motions not amendable

The following motions are not amendable: conclude meeting, terminate meeting, count quorum, point of order, parliamentary inquiry, point of information, question of privilege, withdraw motion, object to consideration, vote immediately, divide motion, rescind, reconsider, make resolution unanimous and motions relating to nominations and elections.[23]

133. Moving an amendment

An amendment may be moved by any person entitled to vote except the chairman of the meeting, the mover (once it has been stated by the chairman) or the seconder of the original motion, or a person who has already spoken on it, unless the meeting consents thereto. It has the same requirements as a motion, is moved and seconded like a motion, and may be amended. The speaker cannot be interrupted in order to move an amendment. It takes precedence over the main motion and a motion to postpone indefinitely. It is debatable unless it is applied to a non-debatable motion. Discussion is limited to the amendment only. It requires the same majority as the original motion.

> *Comment:* Discussion on the original motion is not permissible while an amendment is being discussed. The mover of the original motion may voluntarily accept the amendment and modify his motion accordingly, if there is no objection from the meeting. But once it has been stated by the chairman the motion belongs to the meeting, not to the mover.

> *Motion:* "I move that the motion be amended by adding the words . . . before the word . . ." *or,*

> "I move that the motion be amended by deleting the words . . ." *or,*

> "I move that the motion be amended by substituting the words . . . for the words . . . so that if the amendment is carried the motion will read . . . etc."

---

23 See table inside front cover.

134. Procedure for amending a motion

The procedure for amending a motion is as follows:

1. A motion to amend the motion under discussion is made (Rule 133) and seconded (Rule 125).

2. The chairman considers its relevancy (Rule 127) and its form (Rule 118) and, if satisfied that it is in order, calls for discussion on the amendment.

3. Discussion is opened (Rule 140). If there is any confusion about the wording of the amendment or any doubt as to its exact meaning and effect, the chairman may ask the mover of the amendment to repeat, explain or clarify it.

4. When discussion is ended (Rule 143), the chairman restates the motion to amend and decides upon the method of voting (Rule 153).

5. The vote is taken (Rules 161 to 166).

6. The chairman declares the result (Rule 155).

7. If the motion to amend is defeated or tied, the amendment is dropped and the original motion is proceeded with in the form originally proposed, as if no amendment had been proposed. Another amendment may be proposed and the same procedure followed.

8. If the amendment is carried, the original motion is reworded to incorporate the amendment and is then proceeded with.

SUB-AMENDMENTS

135. Sub-amendments

An amendment may be amended any number of times; but only one amendment to an amendment (sub-amendment) is in order at one time. It must be relevant to the amendment it intends to amend, not to the main motion. The sub-amendment is voted on before the amendment.[24] If the sub-amendment is carried, the original amendment is reworded accordingly. If it is defeated or tied, the sub-amendment is dropped and the original amendment remains on the floor and the amendment is again open for discussion and amendment.

---

24 Rule 134.

136. Moving of sub-amendments

A sub-amendment may be moved by any person entitled to vote at the meeting, except the chairman, the mover or seconder of the original motion and of the amendment, or a person who has already spoken on the original motion or the amendment, unless the meeting consents thereto. In all other respects, the procedure is identical to that for moving an amendment.[25]

137. Voting on sub-amendments

If there is a sub-amendment, it is voted on before the amendment is voted on. If the sub-amendment is carried, the amendment is reworded to incorporate the sub-amendment, and restated by the chairman. Unless another sub-amendment is moved, the amendment is then proceeded with following the procedure for dealing with motions.[26]

Illustration

Motion: "I move that the operations of the company at its Calgary branch be examined by a competent person." (See procedure under Rule 134.)

Amendment No. 1: "I move that the motion be amended by deleting the words 'Calgary branch' and substituting the words 'Calgary and Montreal branches'."

(At this stage no other amendment to the motion may be made, but a sub-amendment to the amendment is permissible.)

Sub-amendment No. 1: "I move that the amendment to the motion be amended by deleting the words 'Calgary and Montreal branches' and substituting the words 'all the branches'."

(Assuming both the amendment and the sub-amendment are carried, the motion now reads as follows: "That the operations of the company at all its branches be examined by a competent person".

At this stage the motion may again be amended.)

Amendment No. 2: "I move that the motion be amended by deleting the words 'a competent person' and substituting the words 'a business consultant'."

---

[25] Rule 133.
[26] Rule 116.

(This amendment could not have been considered while Sub-amendment No. 1 or Amendment No. 1 were on the floor. Amendment No. 2 may now be proceeded with.

Assuming Amendment No. 2 is carried, the motion now reads as follows: "That the operations of the company at all its branches be examined by a business consultant".)

Amendment No. 3: "I move that the motion be amended by adding the words 'selected by the chairman' after the words 'business consultant'."

(Amendment No. 3 cannot be considered until Amendment No. 2 has been dispensed with.

Assuming that all the amendments are carried, the motion now reads: "That the operations of the company at all its branches be examined by a business consultant selected by the chairman".

When this motion is carried, it becomes a resolution: "RESOLVED THAT the operations of the company at all its branches be examined by a business consultant selected by the chairman".)

DISCUSSION

GENERALLY

138. Discussion

Every person entitled to vote has an inherent right to speak and to be heard without interruption. This right may be superseded only by another person entitled to vote who desires to make a motion or a demand which has a higher order of precedence than the motion or demand under discussion.[1]

139. Discussion and debate

Discussion on a debatable motion (or an amendment thereto) is carried on under the supervision of the chairman in accordance with rules of order. The discussion must be relevant to the subject, impersonal and directed to the chairman. In the case of an amendment discussion must be limited to the amendment — not to the motion. If the speaker fails to adhere strictly to the subject under discussion in a courteous, expeditious manner, or otherwise violates the rules of order, he shall be warned. If he persists, the chairman shall rule him out of order and he loses the floor.[2]

140. Opening discussion

Discussion on a debatable motion shall not commence until the motion has been properly moved, seconded and stated by the

---

[1] See Rules 149, 150, and inside front cover.
[2] See Rule 141.

chairman. Before stating the question, the chairman must decide its validity and relevancy.[3] In stating the question, the chairman repeats the motion and invites discussion.

> *Comment:* Sometimes, in small meetings, the subject is discussed before it is put in the form of a motion, and the motion is formulated to conform with the sense of the meeting. This practice is not recommended, as the discussion may tend to get out of control.

141. The floor

A voter wishing to speak raises his hand or otherwise conveys to the chairman his desire to speak, but he does not speak until recognized by the chairman. When recognized, he has the floor and may stand and speak. If several voters request the floor simultaneously, the chairman determines the order in which they are to speak. If the chairman rules a speaker out of order, he loses the floor and shall discontinue speaking and take his seat. A speaker shall yield the floor temporarily for any motion or demand for which the speaker may be interrupted.[4] If he wishes to retain the floor he should remain standing while the chairman deals with the interruption.

> *Comment:* If several voters request the floor simultaneously, the chairman should give priority to the one likely to have a view opposite to the view of the previous speaker.

142. Speakers

Every voter has the right to speak once on each motion and once on each amendment. The mover may not speak against the motion (but he may vote against it). He may speak a second time to explain his motion, answer questions and close the discussion (reply) on his motion. With the consent of the meeting, any voter, including the mover, may have another opportunity to speak. The seconder has no right of reply except with the consent of the meeting. The time for discussion and the length of speeches may be limited within reason by the chairman or by the meeting. However, the rights of minorities to be heard must not be suppressed.[5]

---

[3] See Rule 127.

[4] Rule 149. See inside front cover.

[5] *Const. v. Harris* (1824), Turn. & R. 496, 37 E.R. 1191; *Wall v. London & Northern Assets Corp.*, [1898] 2 Ch. 469.

Comment: It is advisable for every speaker to indicate at the beginning and at the end of his statement whether he is "for" or "against" the motion or amendment.

143. Closing the discussion

When discussion has ended, or on the moving and seconding of a non-debatable motion, the chairman may call for a vote. He should be careful not to stifle debate. Everyone entitled to vote should be permitted to speak. If discussion has continued for a reasonable time and viewpoints for and against have been given, the chairman may ask for a motion to terminate the discussion or vote immediately.[6]

Form: "All in favour of closing discussion, say 'Aye'." "Any against, say 'No'."

DEFERRING DISCUSSION

144. Adjourn discussion

A motion to adjourn discussion, if carried, defers consideration of the main motion until the time fixed by the motion. A speaker may not be interrupted for this motion. It requires seconding and is amendable only as to date and time of adjournment. Debate is restricted to the wisdom of deferring discussion and as to the date and time for resumption of the discussion. This motion requires the same majority as the main motion to which it applied.[7] When discussion on the motion resumes, the mover of the motion has the right to re-open the discussion.

Comment: When a motion to adjourn the meeting to a fixed time has been moved, or more urgent business has arisen, a motion to adjourn discussion on a pending motion is in order. If discussion has not yet commenced, this motion may be called a motion to postpone discussion.

Motion: "I move that consideration of the motion to . . . be adjourned until . . . (*date or event*)" *or* "I move that this meeting adjourn until 2:00 p.m. tomorrow, and the discussion on the motion on the floor be adjourned until the meeting reconvenes."

---

6 Rule 148.
7 Rule 152.

145. Postpone indefinitely

A motion to postpone indefinitely, if carried, defers discussion on the motion and shelves it without a vote. A speaker may not be interrupted for this motion. It requires seconding and is not amendable. Debate is restricted to the advisability of postponing indefinitely. It has no precedence except over the main motion and amendments and applies only to main motions. Only motions to withdraw[8] or vote immediately[9] can be applied to it. It requires the same majority as the main motion to which it is applied.[10]

> *Comment:* This motion has the same effect and characteristics as a motion to shelve, or to proceed to the next business. It is equivalent to a negative vote on the main motion without having it voted upon. The main motion may be renewed at any future meeting.

> *Motion:* "I move that the motion to . . . be postponed indefinitely" (*or* "that further discussion on this motion be postponed indefinitely", *or* "that the meeting proceed to the next order of business", *or* "that this motion be shelved".)

146. Refer or refer back

A motion to refer, if carried, refers the question to the board or a committee for consideration or reconsideration and report. A speaker may not be interrupted for this motion. It requires seconding and is not amendable except for special instructions to the board or committee. Debate is restricted to the propriety of referring the question. It has no precedence except over the main motion and amendments, and applies only to main motions. Only motions to withdraw (Rule 128) or vote immediately (Rule 148) can be applied to it. It requires the same majority as the main motion to which it is applied (Rule 104).

> *Comment:* This motion may have attached to it an appointment of the committee. The matter may be one that the board or committee has already considered, in which case it is a motion to refer back. It may be used as a means of deferring consideration on the motion for the time being.

> *Motion:* "I move that the matter of . . . be referred to the board (*or* the finance committee) for consideration and

---

8 Rule 128.
9 Rule 148.
10 Rule 110.

report." "I move that the matter of . . . be referred to a committee consisting of Mr. A. and Mr. B. for consideration and report."

AVOIDING DISCUSSION

147. Object to consideration

A demand objecting to the consideration of a motion shall be put to a vote immediately. If it is carried, it stops discussion on the main motion. It can be moved only before the first speaker has concluded his remarks. A speaker may be interrupted for this demand. It does not require seconding and is not amendable or debatable. It takes precedence over all motions except closing motions (Rule 173). It can apply to all main motions and can have no other motions applied to it except a motion to withdraw (Rule 128). It must be voted on immediately and requires the same majority as the original motion to which it is applied (Rule 152).

> *Comment:* This demand avoids discussion on a motion which may be inopportune, embarrassing, contentious or unnecessary and which the chairman has failed or refused to rule out of order.

> *Motion:* "I object to the consideration of this motion." (*Reasons may be added in brief.*)

148. Vote immediately

A motion to vote immediately or to close discussion, if carried, stops all discussion, prevents additional amendments being attached to the main motion and brings the motion to an immediate vote. A speaker cannot be interrupted for this motion. It requires seconding, is not amendable or debatable. It takes precedence over all subsidiary motions. It can be applied to all debatable motions and can have no motions applied to it except a motion to withdraw. It requires the same majority as the original motion to which it applies (Rules 106-108).

> *Comment:* This motion is a device for securing a speedy decision.[11] It is also called "close discussion", "closure", "calling the question", "putting the question" and "previous question". If this motion is carried, the main motion is

---

11 *Wall v. The London & Northern* [1898] 2 Ch. 469.

put to a vote without further discussion. If the closure motion is defeated, discussion continues. The chairman is not obligated to accept this motion if he feels that the views of the minority have not been fully aired. The chairman may declare discussion closed even without a motion, when it appears to him that all views have been stated and the meeting acquiesces to closure.

Before closure is voted upon, the chairman should explain that a "Yes" vote on this motion is not a vote in favour of or against the main motion. It is merely a vote to stop discussion. A "No" vote continues discussion.

Motion: "I move that a vote be taken immediately." "I move that discussion close and a vote be taken immediately."

INTERRUPTING DISCUSSION

149. Interrupting a speaker

A speaker who properly has the floor[12] may not be interrupted, except by a person qualified to vote who wishes to make one of the following motions or demands:

(1) Point of order (Rule 92);

(2) Parliamentary inquiry (Rule 93);

(3) Point of information (Rule 94);

(4) Question of privilege (Rule 95);

(5) Object to consideration (Rule 147).

Comment: A voter who wishes to make a motion or demand for which the speaker may be interrupted may say: "Point of order, Mr. Chairman", or "Mr. Chairman, I rise to a point of order". (See also Rule 141.)

150. Interrupting discussion

Interrupting discussion is changing the subject of the motion on the floor. The discussion may not be interrupted except by a person qualified to vote who wishes to make one of the following motions or demands:

(1) Conclude meeting (Rule 173);

(2) Terminate meeting (Rule 173);

---

[12] Rule 141.

(3) Adjourn to a fixed day (Rule 174);

(4) Recess (Rule 175);

(5) Count quorum (Rule 83);

(6) Point of order (Rule 92);

(7) Parliamentary inquiry (Rule 93);

(8) Point of information (Rule 94);

(9) Question of privilege (Rule 95);

(10) Withdraw motion (Rule 128);

(11) Object to consideration (Rule 147);

(12) Vote immediately (Rule 148);

(13) Adjourn discussion (Rule 144);

(14) Postpone indefinitely (Rule 145);

(15) Refer or refer back (Rule 146);

(16) Amend motion (Rule 133);

(17) Divide a motion (Rules 120, 121).

CHAPTER VII

SENSE OF THE MEETING

GENERALLY

151. Sense of the meeting

It is the duty of the chairman to ascertain the sense of the meeting[1] with regard to all questions properly brought before it, and to decide all questions which require decision at the time.[2]

Comment: The chairman's rulings approximate those of a person occupying a judicial[3] or quasi judicial[4] position.

152. Majority vote

Unless there are provisions to the contrary in the governing statute or the constitution, all ordinary questions are decided by a majority of votes.[5] If the meeting is duly convened and a proper resolution is duly passed by the required majority,[6] the vote is binding on the minority.

Comment: Shares of those not voting are not counted.

---

[1] *Gray v. Yellowknife Gold Mines Ltd.,* [1946] O.W.N. 938; *Re LeMay Ltd.* (1924) 26 O.W.N. 443; *Henderson v. Bank of Australasia* (1890) 45 Ch. D. 330 (C.A.); *National Dwellings Society v. Sykes,* [1894] 3 Ch. 159; *Re Indian Zoedone Co.* (1884), 26 Ch. D. 70; *Cornwall and Pain v. Woods* (1846), 4 Notes of Cases 555.

[2] *Re Indian Zoedone, supra.*

[3] *Bluechel and Smith v. Prefabricated Buildings Ltd. and Thomas,* [1945] 2 D.L.R. 725.

[4] *Gray v. Yellowknife Gold Mines Ltd., supra.*

[5] Rules 6, 106.

[6] Rules 106, 107 and 108.

153. Methods of voting

The chairman shall ascertain the sense of the meting by one of the following methods:

(1) Acquiescence (Rule 154);

(2) Voice vote (Rule 161);

(3) Show of hands (Rule 162);

(4) Ballot (Rules 163, 164, 165).

Comment: The most accurate method of voting is by ballot. All other methods are imperfect substitutes and are used only when there is little doubt as to the probable result of the vote.

154. Acquiescence

If the chairman feels that the meeting is unanimous in its opinion on the question, and there is no objection, he may assume that the shareholders approve of his action or statement. If any objection is voiced the chairman calls for a voice vote, a show of hands or a ballot.

Chairman: "Are there any corrections (to the minutes)? Hearing none, the minutes will stand verified as read." "If no one objects, we will proceed with the meeting (*or* "consider the matter approved," *or* "rejected" *or* "terminated.")

155. Chairman's decision

The chairman shall declare the result of the vote without delay.[7] A declaration by the chairman that a resolution has been carried and an entry to that effect in the minutes of the meeting constitute *prima facie* evidence of the fact without proof of the number or proportion of the votes recorded in favour of or against the resolution.[8]

Comment: Such a declaration is only *prima facie* evidence and is not conclusive,[9] but it is binding unless overruled by the court.[10] See Rule 70.

---

[7] Rule 168.

[8] *Arnot v. United African Lands, Ltd.,* [1901] 1 Ch. 518; *Re Hadleigh Castle Gold Mines, Ltd.,* [1900] 2 Ch. 419.

[9] *Colonial Ass'ce Co. v. Smith* (1912), 4 D.L.R. 814; *Wall v. Exchange Investment Corp., Ltd.,* [1926] 1 Ch. 143.

[10] *Re Indian Zoedone Co.* (1884), 26 Ch. D. 70; *Arnot v. United African Lands Ltd., supra; Young v. South African and Australian Exploration & Development Syndicate,* [1896] 2 Ch. 268.

RIGHTS OF SHAREHOLDERS

156. Shareholders right to vote

Unless the constitution or the statute[11] provides otherwise[12] every shareholder is entitled to one vote for every share registered in his name.[13]

> *Comment:* Holding a share certificate endorsed in blank does not qualify the holder to vote. Some statutes and some constitutions have provisions in this regard. Some corporations provide for voting certificates whereby the holder of bearer certificates or share certificates endorsed in blank may deposit them with the company or its transfer registrar and receive a voting certificate entitling him to vote at a specific meeting. After the meeting his certificates will be returned to him.

157. Manner of voting

Every person entitled to vote (including the mover and seconder) may vote in favour of the motion or against the motion or may refrain from voting, provided that in so doing he commits no fraud.

> *Comment:* A voter may vote as he pleases regardless of his personal interest[14] or the possible consequences of the vote, provided that he is not disqualified from voting, that no

---

11 In some jurisdictions persons not being beneficial owners may be prohibited from voting on such shares. Regulations of some exchanges restrict brokers from voting shares not beneficially owned by them.

12 The question of beneficial ownership cannot be entered into. (*Pender v. Lushington* (1877), 6 Ch. D. 70.) See Rule 174.

13 *Tough Oakes Gold Mines Ltd. v. Foster* (1917), 34 D.L.R. 748.

14 "There is no obligation on a shareholder to give his vote merely with a view to what other persons may consider the interests of the company at large. He has a right, if he thinks fit, to give his vote from motives or promptings of what he considers his own interest." (Jessel, M. R., in *Pender v. Lushington, supra); Menier v. Hooper's Telegraph Works* (1874), 9 Ch. App. 350. "In the absence of fraud, the right of shareholders to be swayed in their vote at shareholders' meetings by their own personal interest is well established." (*Garvie v. Axmith* (1961), 31 D.L.R. (2d) 65.) "Unless some provision to the contrary is to be found in the charter or other instrument by which the company is incorporated, the resolution of a majority of the shareholders, duly convened, upon any question with which the company is legally competent to deal, is binding on the minority, and consequently upon the company, and every shareholder has a perfect right to vote upon such questions, although he may have a personal interest in the subject matter opposed to or different from the general or particular interests of the company." (*North-West Transportation Co. Ltd. v. Beatty* (1887), 12 App. Cas. 589 at p. 593; rev'g 12 S.C.R. 598.) See also *Western Ontario Natural Gas Co. Ltd. v. Aikens*, [1946] 4 D.L.R. 647; *Stockford v. McPherson* (1916), 9 W.W.R. 1192; *Ritchie v. Vermillion Mining Co.* (1902), 4 O.L.R. 588; *MacDonald Bros. v. Godson* (1916), 31 D.L.R. 363; *Elliott v. Richardson* (1870), L.R. 5 C.P. 744; *Re London & Mercantile Discount Co.* (1865), L.R. 1 Eq. 277.

fraud is committed against the minority in consequence of the vote, and that the company is not deprived of its assets.[15] While he may vote as he pleases, he must exercise his vote in the interests of the class.[16] The courts will not invalidate a shareholder's vote merely because he has a personal interest in the subject matter different from or opposed to that of the company.[17]

158. Joint holders

Joint holders of shares must concur in voting upon them unless the constitution provides otherwise.[18] Joint holders present at a meeting of shareholders may in the absence of the other or others, vote on these shares, but if more than one of them are present or represented by proxy, they shall vote together.[19] Executors and trustees must all concur in voting the shares of the estate they represent.[18]

159. Votes are open

Every voter has the right to know how every other voter voted.

Comment: There is no such thing as a secret vote in company meetings.[20]

160. Changing vote

A shareholder has a right to change his vote up to the time the result of the vote is declared by the chairman if the vote is by voice or a show of hands, or, if a poll is taken, up to the time his ballot is handed to the chairman or scrutineer.

---

15 See Rule 6. Directors holding a majority of votes could not be permitted to make a present to themselves; this would allow a majority to oppress a minority (*Cood v. Deeks* (1916), 27 D.L.R. 1, rev'g 21 D.L.R. 497). *Lumbers v. Fretz*, [1928] 4 D.L.R. 269, 854; aff'd [1929] 1 D.L.R. 51; *Menier v. Hooper's Telegraph Works* (1874), 9 Ch. App. 350; *Ritchie v. Vermillion Mining Co.* (1902) 4 O.L.R. 588.

16 Where his vote is conferred on him as a member of a class he is bound to exercise it in the interest of the class itself (*British American Nickel Corp., Ltd. v. O'Brien*, [1927] A.C. 369; aff'g [1925] 4 D.L.R. 455).

17 He has a perfect right to exercise his voting power in such a manner as to secure the election of directors whose views upon policy agree with his own, and to support those at any shareholders' meeting (*North-West Transportation Co. Ltd. v. Beatty* (1877), 12 App. Cas. 589); *Montreal Trust Co. v. Oxford Pipe Line* [1942] O.R. 490.

18 *Lumbers v. Fretz, supra.* See Rule 21.

19 Saskatchewan: *Business Corporations Act*, R.S.S. 1978, c. B-10, s. 134(4). Manitoba: *Corporations Act*, S.M. 1976, c. 40, s. 134(3). Ontario: *Business Corporations Act*, 1982, s. 102(4). New Brunswick: *Business Corporations Act*, N.B.A. 1981, c. B-9.1, s. 93(4).

20 "No method of voting is better than that of open declaration." (Cicero: *De Legibus*).

VOTING AND POLLS

161. Voice vote

A vote by voice is a simple and quick method of voting. If the chairman has any doubt as to the result, he should take a poll.

> *Chairman:* "All in favour, say: 'Aye'. Any opposed, say: 'No'."

> *Comment:* A vote by voice is an imperfect method of voting and is not recommended except where the vote is unquestionably one-sided.

162. Show of hands

A vote by show of hands is conclusive where a poll is not demanded and the chairman declares the result.[21] If there is any doubt as to the result, the chairman should take a poll. The shareholders present vote only for themselves, not for the absent shareholders whom they represent by proxy.[22] Proxyholders who are not shareholders may vote for their principals.[23]

> *Comment:* A show of hands, although quick and simple, is only a crude and imperfect method of ascertaining the sentiments of the electors.[24] It stands as the resolution of the meeting unless displaced by a poll duly demanded and taken.[25]

163. Demanding a poll

Every person having the right to vote has the right to demand a poll.[26] A proxyholder is not qualified to demand a poll unless he

---

21 *Re Horbury Bridge Coal, Iron & Waggon Co.* (1879), 11 Ch. D. 109; *Carruth v. Imperial Chemical Industries, Ltd.*, [1937] A.C. 707: "A show of hands is the constitutional method of declaring the will of the meeting".

22 *Anthony v. Seger* (1789), 1 Hag. Con. 9, 161 E.R. 457.

23 "On a show of hands, a person holding proxies, if he is a shareholder, has one vote, but only one for himself and all the shareholders whom he represents; if a person who is not a shareholder, being permitted under the company's regulations to act as proxy, represents only one person, *viz*: the absentee from whom he votes, apparently he can vote on a show of hands" (*Ernest v. Loma Gold Mines, Ltd.*, [1896] 2 Ch. 572; aff'd [1897] 1 Ch. 1).

24 Where the vote is on a show of hands, a shareholder representing an absent shareholder as a proxy votes only for himself. Consequently his vote will not operate as an estoppel against the absent shareholder. *McKenna v. Spooner Oils Ltd.*, [1934] 1 W.W.R. 255; *Ernest v. Loma Gold Mines, Ltd.*, [1897] 1 Ch. 1; *Pacific Coast Coal Mines Ltd. v. Arbuthnot* (1917), 36 D.L.R. 564.

25 *Carruth v. Imperial Chemical Industries Ltd.* [1937] A.C. 707: "A show of hands is the constitutional method of declaring the will of the meeting."

26 *Ernest v. Loma Gold Mines Ltd., supra; Campbell v. Maund* (1836), 5 Ad. & E. 865, 111 E.R. 1394; *R. v. Wimbledon Local Board* (1882), 8 Q.D.B. 459; *Re Phoenix Electric Light & Power Co.* (1883), 31 W.R. 398.

has the authority under the document appointing him.[27] The chairman may direct a poll without taking a show of hands.[28] A demand for a poll must be made as soon as the show of hands is over.[29] When a poll is demanded, it nullifies a vote by show of hands.[30] Once a demand for a poll has been made, it cannot be withdrawn without the consent of the meeting and if the poll is not taken after a proper demand for it, the resolution is void.[31]

> *Comment:* It is often advisable for the chairman to direct a poll without taking a show of hands, especially if in his opinion a show of hands does not give a true indication of the sense of the meeting, as may be the case where many shareholders are represented by proxyholders.

164. Mandatory poll

A poll must be taken on any motion that requires more than a simple majority of the votes cast, unless the vote is unanimous.

165. Procedure for taking poll

The poll shall be taken by roll call or by ballot as the chairman directs or the constitution provides. The procedure may be as follows:

1. A ballot is handed to every person entitled to vote. It may be either blank paper or a printed ballot (see Forms 19, 20, 21).

2. The voters are instructed to write "FOR" or "AGAINST" on the ballot or, if the ballot is printed, to mark an "X" opposite the appropriate word.

3. The voters are instructed to write their names at the foot of the ballot, and, if voting by proxy, to add the words "For self and those who appoint me their proxyholder," or, "on behalf of . . ." giving name(s) of shareholder(s), or words to that effect.

4. The chairman collects the ballots, examines them, decides their validity (Rule 167), counts the votes cast and declares the result (Rule 168). The chairman's decision stands unless reversed by the court.

---

27 *Re Haven Gold Mining Co.* (1881), 20 Ch. D. 151.

28 *R. v. Birmingham (Rector)* (1837), 7 Ad. & E. 254, 112 E.R. 467; *Second Consolidated Trust Ltd. v. Ceylon Amalgamated Tea & Rubber Estates, Ltd.,* [1943] 2 All E.R. 567.

29 *Campbell v. Maund, supra; R. v. Thomas* (1883), 11 Q.B.D. 282.

30 *Anthony v. Seger* (1789), 1 Hagg Con. 9, 161 E.R. 457.

31 *R. v. Cooper* (1870), L.R. 5 Q.B. 457.

5. The chairman may appoint scrutineers to assist him in collecting, examining and counting the votes, but only he may rule on the validity of the ballots and declare the result (Rule 168).

166. When poll to be taken

When a poll is demanded, it shall be taken forthwith. If the poll is on the election of a chairman or on a motion to adjourn, the votes shall be counted forthwith, and the result declared before any further business is conducted.[32] On any other question the count may be made at such time as the chairman directs, and other business may be proceeded with pending the results of the poll. Up to the time the poll is declared closed and the chairman (or the scrutineers) begin examining ballots, any person qualified to vote may vote.[33]

Comment: The U.S. Supreme Court held that balloting can continue until the results have been officially announced.[34]

BALLOTS

167. Validity of ballots

A ballot is valid only if:

(1) It is intelligible and indicates the clear intention of the person casting it;

(2) It is cast and signed by a shareholder qualified to vote on the question or his duly appointed proxyholder;

(3) It is marked for or against a question, for or against a motion for appointment, or for a candidate for election; and

(4) In the case of a proxyholder who is, by the document appointing him, restricted in voting on the question, he votes in accordance with his instructions.

168. Counting ballots

It is the duty of the chairman to examine all ballots, decide on their validity, count the votes cast and declare the result.[35] His declaration as to the result of the vote is final and binding unless reversed by the court. He may delegate to scrutineers[36] the exami-

---

[32] Rules 155, 168.

[33] *Campbell v. Maund* (1836), 5 Ad. & E. 364, 111 E.R. 1394; *R. v. Wimbledon Local Board* (1882), 8 Q.B.D. 459.

[34] *Washington State Labour Council v. Federated American Insurance Co.* (S.C. 1970) 474 P 2d 98.

[35] Rules 155, 167.

[36] Rule 78.

nation of the ballots, the consideration of their validity and the counting, but he may adopt or reject the scrutineers' report[37] in whole or in part.

169. Possession of ballots

Ballots, on being deposited with the company, become records of the company. The chairman, scrutineers and voters may examine ballots at any reasonable time, during or after the meeting.

> *Comment:* The same rule applies to proxies (Rule 197). Adequate precautions should be taken to prevent any tampering with or disappearance of ballots (and proxies) so long as the possibility of controversy exists.

---

[37] *Dickson v. McMurray* (1881), 28 Gr. 533.

CHAPTER VIII

CLOSING THE MEETING

GENERALLY

170. Closing the meeting

Closing motions are motions to:

— conclude the meeting (all business is completed);[1]

— terminate the meeting or adjourn *sine die* (cancels all unfinished business);

— adjourn to a fixed time (to resume unfinished business at the time fixed);[2]

— recess (for a short time).[3]

Closing motions, if defeated, cannot be repeated until after other business has intervened. Motions to close the meeting have the highest precedence of any motion.[4]

> *Comment:* The chairman and the meeting should make every effort to continue the meeting until all business is concluded. The chairman need not accept a motion to adjourn if in his opinion it is an abuse of privilege or is being

[1] Rule 173.
[2] Rule 174.
[3] Rule 175.
[4] Rule 114 and table inside front cover.

moved merely to obstruct business. It is the chairman's duty to continue the meeting until all its business has been concluded. (See Rule 65.)

171. When out of order

While a motion to adjourn has the highest priority of any motion it cannot be moved:

— when someone has the floor;

— while a point of order, parliamentary inquiry, point of information or question of privilege is being considered;

— immediately after a similar motion has been defeated and no other business has intervened;

— when another version of the motion to adjourn is on the floor; or

— in the case of a motion to terminate, while a vote is being taken or ballots are being counted.

172. When debatable and amendable

A motion to close the meeting is not debatable or amendable, but a motion to adjourn to a fixed day or to recess is debatable and amendable as to time and place only.

MOTIONS

173. Motion to conclude or terminate

A motion to conclude (when all business is finished) or a motion to terminate (when business is not finished) if passed, dissolves the meeting completely. Discussion may be interrupted for this purpose, but not while a speaker has the floor. It requires seconding and is not amendable or debatable. A motion to conclude or terminate has the highest precedence of any motion, applies to no other motion and can have no other motion applied to it except a motion to withdraw. It requires a simple majority.

> *Comment:* A motion to terminate is the same as a motion to adjourn *sine die* (without fixing a day). They both dissolve the meeting and cancel out all unfinished business and pending matters (Rule 170).

174. Motion to adjourn to a fixed day

This motion, if passed, suspends the meeting to reconvene on the day fixed. It has no effect on the agenda. The discussion may

be interrupted for this purpose, but not while a speaker has the
floor. It requires seconding and is not amendable or debatable,[5]
except as to time and place. A motion to adjourn has the highest
precedence of any motion.[6] It applies to no other motion and can
have no motion applied to it except a motion to withdraw. It
requires a simple majority.

> *Comment:* If no date is fixed, the motion may be deemed to
> be a motion to terminate or conclude.

> *Motion:* "I move that this meeting adjourn to reconvene on
> [*date*] at [*hour*] at [*place*]."

175. Motion to recess

This motion, if passed, suspends the meeting for a short time
(usually not more than one hour) to reconvene on the same day.
It has no effect on the agenda. The discussion may be interrupted
for this purpose, but not while a speaker has the floor. It requires
seconding and is not amendable or debatable[7] except as to the time
to reconvene. It takes precedence[8] over all motions except other
closing motions. It applies to no other motion and can have no
motion applied to it except a motion to amend (as to time) and a
motion to withdraw. It requires a simple majority.

> *Motion:* "I move that this meeting recess, to reconvene at
> [*time*]."

176. Adjournment by the chairman

The chairman may, with the consent of the meeting, adjourn
the meeting from time to time and from place to place according
to such conditions as the meeting may determine. The chairman
has no power to close the meeting without the consent of the meeting[9] except where discussion has degenerated and the transaction
of business has become impossible,[10] where a quorum is lacking,[11]
or when all the business of the meeting has been concluded.

---

[5] See Rule 172.
[6] See Rule 114.
[7] See Rule 172.
[8] See Rule 114.
[9] *Salisbury Gold Mining Co. Ltd. v. Hathorn*, [1897] A.C. 268.
[10] Should the chairman pronounce the adjournment when the meeting,
though unruly, is not so agitated as to justify the adjournment, another chairman may continue its proceedings and conclude the unfinished business
(*National Dwellings Society v. Sykes*, [1894] 3 Ch. 159).
[11] Rule 86.

Comment: If the chairman has properly adjourned the meeting, it cannot be continued by a group of voters who remain behind.[12] If he has improperly vacated the chair[13] or adjourned the meeting, it may be continued by the voters who remain who shall elect another chairman (Rule 65).

RESULT OF ADJOURNMENT

177. Improper adjournment

If the chairman improperly closes the meeting,[14] leaves the chair,[15] or disqualifies himself by his actions,[16] the voters may elect a new chairman and continue with the unfinished business.

Comment: The chairman and the meeting should exert every effort to continue the meeting until all business is concluded.

178. Waiving irregularity

By participating in an adjourned meeting, the voters are deemed to have waived any irregularity in the adjournment.[17]

179. Adjourned meeting, continuation

The adjourned meeting is deemed to be a continuation of the meeting.[18] The chairman who presided at the original meeting is entitled to preside at the adjourned meeting.[19]

180. Adjourned meeting, business

No new business not covered in the notice of the original meeting may be transacted unless a new and proper notice is given.[20]

---

[12] *R. v. Gaborian* (1809), 11 East 77, 103 E.R. 933.

[13] *Catesby v. Burnett* [1916] 2 Ch. 325; *Gray v. Yellowknife Gold Mines Ltd.*, [1946] O.W.N. 938.

[14] *National Dwellings Society v. Sykes, supra.*

[15] *Catesby v. Burnett,* [1916] 2 Ch. 325.

[16] Rule 65. "Where the chairman is obstructing the continuation of the meeting, the shareholders should pass a motion to adjourn and convene at a specified time either immediately after in the same room or an adjacent room, or at some other specified place" (*Salisbury Gold Mining Co. Ltd. v. Hathorn, supra*).

[17] *Gray v. Yellowknife Gold Mines Ltd.*, [1946] O.W.N. 938.

[18] *Spencer v. Kennedy* [1926] Ch. 125, 135; *Neuschild v. British Equatorial Oil Co. Ltd.*, [1925] Ch. 346; *McLaren v. Thomson,* [1917] 2 Ch. 261; *Scadding v. Lorant* (1851), 3 H.L. Cas 418; *Wills v. Murray* (1850), 4 Exch. 843.

[19] *Dominion Royalty Corp. v. Holbourn* (1932), 41 O.W.N. 288. See Rule 17.

[20] See Rule 57. See also Rule 225 for the deposit of proxy forms. *Christopher v. Noxon* (1884) 4 O.R. 672; *McLaren v. Thomson* [1917] 2 Ch. 261.

CHAPTER IX

MINUTES

MINUTES GENERALLY

181. Minutes

Minutes of all proceedings at meetings of shareholders and of the board of directors must be entered in books kept for that purpose.

> *Comment:* Directors ought to place on record, either in formal minutes or otherwise, the purpose and effect of their deliberations and conclusions. If they do this insufficiently or inaccurately they cannot reasonably complain if false inferences are drawn from their reports.[1]

182. Form

Minutes should contain date, time and place of meeting, persons present, names of chairman and secretary, resolutions passed, appointments made and business conducted[2] and should be signed by the chairman of the meeting, or by the chairman of the next meeting at which they are verified.

---

1 *Re Liverpool Household Stores Ass'n* (1890), 59 L.J. Ch. 616, at p. 619.

2 Minutes need not contain speeches, arguments or motions that were not passed (*Boston Shoe Co. Ltd. v. Frank* (1915), 48 Que. S.C. 66). A minute is not a report. A "report" is what was said at the meeting, *e.g.*, a stenographer's transcript comprising speeches and arguments. A "minute" is what was done or agreed upon, *e.g.*, resolutions and decisions.

183. Minutes as proof of meeting

When the minutes are signed, the meeting is deemed to have been duly called, constituted and held, unless the court determines otherwise. Unless and until refuted,[3] such minutes and the resolutions therein set out are deemed to be true and accurate.

> *Comment:* Minutes may be contradicted or proved by parol evidence.[4] The *prima facie* proof of signed minutes may be contradicted by parol evidence of persons who were present at the meeting.[5] The passage of unrecorded resolutions may be proved by parol or other evidence.[6] Unsigned minutes will not prevent their being used as evidence.[7]

184. Minutes as evidence in court

Minutes are admissible in Court[8] as *prima facie* proof:

(1) that the meeting was held on the date shown;

(2) that the persons described as being present were actually present;

(3) that the transactions described were in fact made at the meeting.

> *Comment:* The Court is not always prepared to accept minutes as *prima facie* evidence of oral statements attributed to persons present.[9]

---

3 "The minutes in the books are to be received, not as conclusive, but as *prima facie* evidence of resolutions and proceedings at general meetings. The entry of the minutes in the books though in no sense conclusive, throws the burden of proof upon the other side, who may say, contrary to the entry on the minute book following the decision of the chairman, that the result of the poll was different from that there recorded." (*Re Indian Zoedone Co.* (1884), 26 Ch. D. 70.)

4 Evidence may be given to show what in fact was done even if this contradicts the minutes (*Re Fireproof Doors Ltd.,* [1916] 2 Ch. 142; *Wilson v. Woollatt,* [1929] S.C.R. 483; *Fullerton v. Crawford* (1919), 59 S.C.R. 314).

5 *Bartlett v. Bartlett Mines Ltd.* (1911), 24 O.L.R. 419; *Hood and Snow v. Eden* (1905), 36 S.C.R. 476; *Re Great Northern Salt and Chemical Works, Ex p. Kennedy* (1889), 44 Ch. D. 472; *Re Pyle Works Co.* (No. 2), [1891] 1 Ch. 173.

6 *Re Fireproof Doors Ltd., supra.*

7 *Re S. Medine & Co. Ltd.; Trustee v. Rasminsky* (1925), 7 C.B.R. 578, *Associated Stevedoring v. Callanan* (1968) 70 D.L.R. (2d) 687; *Wilson v. Woollatt* [1928] 62 O.L.R. 620.

8 Under Section 35 of the *Evidence Act* (Ontario).

9 *Setak Computer v. Burroughs* 15 O.R. (2d) 750; *Fullerton v. Crawford* (1919) 59 S.C.R. 314 reversing *Crawford v. Bathurst* 1918 O.L.R. 256.

PREVIOUS MEETINGS

185. Minutes of previous meeting

The minutes of a previous meeting may be verified by the signature of the chairman of such meeting, or by the signature of the chairman or secretary of a subsequent meeting after a resolution to verify has been passed. Discussion on the business of the previous meeting is not in order.[10]

> *Comment:* There does not appear to be any obligation to have minutes verified, but it is considered good practice. The motion does not by itself ratify or adopt the business transacted; it merely verifies the minutes. Only the accuracy of the minutes may be discussed[11] except on a motion to reconsider a resolution passed at a previous meeting.[12] A shareholder does not make himself liable for any illegal act done at a meeting at which he was not present merely by voting subsequently for the verification of the minutes,[13] but he may if he votes for the adoption or ratification of the minutes. Sometimes, particularly with minutes of meetings of private companies, motions to verify have added to them adoption and ratification.

186. Procedure to verify minutes

To verify minutes of a previous meeting:

1. The chairman or the secretary reads the minutes to the meeting.

2. He asks for any errors or omissions. If there is no objection, he may sign the minutes. A declaration of the chairman to the effect that the minutes stand verified is sufficient.

3. If there are objections, the chairman may accept them and direct the secretary to make the necessary changes.

4. If the chairman desires the minutes to be verified by resolution, he asks for a motion to verify. Only persons who were present at the meeting may properly move, second or vote on the motion.

5. The minutes of the meeting will record the verification of the minutes of the previous meeting.

---

10 *R. v. York Corporation* (1853), 1 El. & Bl. 588, 118 E.R. 558.
11 *Ibid.*
12 Rule 123.
13 *Burton v. Bevan,* [1908] 2 Ch. 240.

Chairman: "You have heard the minutes (of the previous meeting). Are there any errors or omissions? If there are no objections I will verify them as correct." *Or,* "The minutes stand verified as read."

(If the chairman desires a motion) "You have heard the minutes. Are there any errors or omissions? Will someone move that the minutes be verified as correct?"

Motion: "I move that the minutes of the meeting of shareholders held . . . (date) be hereby verified."

Amendment: "I move that the motion to verify be amended by adding the words '. . .'," *or*

"I move that the motion to verify be amended by deleting the words '. . .'," *or*

"I move that the motion to verify be amended by deleting the words '. . .' and substituting the words '. . .'."

Comment: A motion to verify may be enlarged to include confirmation and adoption, in which case the persons voting in favour are bound by the minutes of a meeting whether or not they were present at the meeting (see Rule 185). A motion to dispense with the reading may be passed.

187. Alterations

If it is discovered later that the minutes are incorrect, although verified, they may be altered only with the approval of a meeting, preferably the next meeting. Only those who were present at the meeting in question may move, second or vote on the motion to alter the minutes. Minutes should never be altered subsequently[14] or pages removed or added.

---

[14] "I trust I shall never again see or hear of the secretary of a company, whether under superior directions or otherwise, altering minutes of meetings, either by striking out anything or adding anything." (*Re Cawley & Co.* (1889), 42 Ch. D. 209.)

CHAPTER X

PROXIES

PROXIES GENERALLY

188. Right to vote by proxy

The right of shareholders to vote by proxy is a right conferred in some jurisdictions by statute[1] and in other jurisdictions by the constitution.[2]

189. Board to regulate

Subject to the provisions of the governing statute and the constitution, the board determines the form and regulations governing proxy forms.

---

[1] *McLaren v. Thomson,* [1917] 2 Ch. 261; *Sanderson v. Henry* (1904), 16 Que. K.B. 78; *Harben v. Phillips* (1882), 23 Ch. D. 14.

[2] See *Cousins v. International Brick Co., Ltd.,* [1931] 2 Ch. 90.

Comment: The shareholders have no right to initiate any such regulations.[3] It is doubtful whether the court has the authority to regulate proxies.[4]

190. Proxies

The proxies must comply with the statute and the constitution as well as with securities acts and regulations.

Comment: In some jurisdictions the inclusion of extraneous material invalidates the proxy. This was the case in Ontario up to 1966[5] and is still the case in Quebec.

191. Chairman decides validity

The chairman examines all proxies and decides their validity and the qualifications of the appointees.[6] His decision is final and binding[7] unless reversed by the court. He may delegate to scrutineers[8] the examination of the proxies and consideration of their validity, but he is not obligated to adopt the scrutineers' report. Before a vote by proxy is accepted, the chairman shall satisfy himself that:

(1) the appointor has the right to vote at the meeting;

(2) the proxyholder is present[9] and qualified to act as such;

(3) the document appointing him is in proper form and properly signed;

(4) the document has been deposited in time;

(5) the appointment has not been revoked;

---

[3] *Kelly v. Electrical Construction Co.* (1907), 16 O.L.R. 232; *Colonial Ass'ce Co. v. Smith* (1912), 4 D.L.R. 814.

[4] "I find nothing in the statute which authorizes a judge to prescribe anything with reference to proxies" (Middleton, J. A., in *Re Dairy Corp. of Canada Ltd.,* [1934] 3 D.L.R. 347, at p. 349).

[5] *Re National Grocers Co. Ltd.,* [1938] 3 D.L.R. 106; *Re Langley's Ltd.,* [1938] 3 D.L.R. 230; *Montreal Trust Co. v. Oxford Pipe Line Co.,* [1942] 2 D.L.R. 703, aff'd [1942] 3 D.L.R. 619; *Re Western Canada Flour Mills Ltd.,* [1945] 1 D.L.R. 589; *Re N. Slater Co. Ltd.,* [1947] 2 D.L.R. 311.

[6] "Unless other rules are established by by-law, it devolves upon the chairman to examine the instruments of proxy and decide upon their validity and the qualifications of their holders, and his decision is binding unless proved to the court to have been wrong" (*Re Indian Zeodone Co.* (1884), 26 Ch. D. 70). See also *Wall v. London & Northern Assets Corp.,* [1899] 1 Ch. 550; *Wall v. Exchange Investment Corp., Ltd.,* [1926] 1 Ch. 143; *Bluechel and Smith v. Prefabricated Buildings Ltd. and Thomas,* [1945] 2 D.L.R. 725.

[7] See Rule 193.

[8] See Rule 178.

[9] *McMillan v. Le Roi Mining Co., Ltd.,* [1906] 1 Ch. 331.

(6) the vote conforms with the restrictions and instructions contained in the document.

> *Comment:* The chairman is not obligated to accept a form of proxy merely because the same form has been accepted for previous meetings.[10]

192. Proxies deemed valid

Each proxy is deemed to be valid and genuine if the form is proper and it appears to have been executed by a person qualified to vote. The improper rejection or admission of a proxy may invalidate the result of the vote.

> *Comment:* Improper rejection of proxies is a ground for setting aside an election of directors.[11] See Rule 229.

193. Objections

Objections to the acceptance or rejection of proxies must be made at the meeting, otherwise the party objecting may be deemed to have waived any irregularity.[12] Every voter has the right to challenge proxies and ballots and should be given an opportunity to make representations to the chairman before, as well as after, his declaration thereon. No representations may be made to the scrutineers.

194. Authority of proxyholders

Proxyholders are bound by the documents appointing them and the notice convening the meeting. Unless the appointment specifically authorizes them, they cannot vote on any business not included in the notice,[13] or on any modification or amendment to

---

[10] The fact that a particular form of proxy has been accepted by the chairman at previous meetings of the company does not validate an improper form. (*Montreal Trust Co. v. Oxford Pipe Line Co.,* [1942] 2 D.L.R. 703, aff'd [1942] 3 D.L.R. 619.)

[11] *Kelly v. Electrical Construction Co.* (1907), 16 O.L.R. 232; *Re Bidwell Bros.,* [1893] 1 Ch. 603.

[12] "As to the objections not having been taken before the chairman at the meeting, generally speaking, the objection should be taken at the meeting. If not so taken and the ground is one of substance, the court may in its discretion, and under special circumstances, entertain the appeal. Where, however, an appellant intends to rely upon technical objections, he should specifically state his objections at the meeting to the chairman prior to the chairman rendering his decision and have them noted in the minutes of the meeting; unless he so objects, he will be deemed to have waived any irregularity or formal defect and an appeal will not lie from the chairman's decision in regard thereto." (*Re McCoubrey, Ex parte Stratton; Ex parte Greenshields Ltd.; Ex parte W. R. Brock Co. Ltd.,* [1924] 4 D.L.R. 1227.)

[13] *Marks v. Rocsand Co. Ltd.* (1920), 55 D.L.R. 557, rev'd on other grounds 64 D.L.R. 254; *Lumbers v. Fretz,* [1928] 4 D.L.R. 269, 854, aff'd [1929] 1 D.L.R. 51; *Pacific Coast Coal Mines Ltd. v. Arbuthnot* (1917), 36 D.L.R. 564.

any business included in the notice.[14] Proxyholders cannot waive notice of a meeting or any irregularity in the calling or holding of the meeting unless specifically authorized to do so.

195. Solicitation of proxies

The methods used to solicit proxies affect their validity.[15] Proxies obtained without disclosure of the matters to be voted on, or otherwise improperly obtained are invalid, and votes based upon them are nullified.[16]

> *Comment:* If the notice of meeting or soliciting material contains statements which are contrary to law,[17] or are false or misleading, this is an offence against the statute and the person responsible may be liable to a fine or imprisonment or both. Proxies obtained on such material are nullified.[18]

196. Duration of proxy

A document appointing a proxyholder, being a power of attorney, is a contract of agency in writing. Unless statutory restrictions or the terms of the appointment set a limit after which it is invalid, no such time limit exists.

> *Comment:* Some statutes limit the duration of the proxy to one year, others to one specified meeting and adjournments thereof.

---

14 *Re Langley's Ltd.*, [1938] 3 D.L.R. 230.

15 "Those who seek the proxies of their fellow corporate shareholders assume a fiduciary obligation. Failure to make a full disclosure is a breach of fiduciary obligation." *Willoughby v. Port*, 182 F. Supp. 496; aff'd 277 F. 2d 149 (1960).

16 *Pacific Coast Coal Mines Ltd. v. Arbuthnot, supra; Lumbers v. Fretz, supra; Marks v. Rocsand Co. Ltd., supra.* Where proxies had been obtained from shareholders without acquainting them with what was proposed to be voted on or giving them reasonable information to enable them to decide whether or not they should be present in person it was held to be "an abuse of the powers given to" the proxy (*Lumbers v. Fretz, supra,* following *Pacific Coast Coal Mines Ltd. v. Arbuthnot, supra; Fullerton v. Crawford* (1919), 59 S.C.R. 314). "The printed names of three directors who were promoters of the scheme were filled in and accompanied by a marginal note: 'If you desire to nominate any other person your proxy, strike out the printed name and fill in the name of your nominee.' I think this is vicious and may have influenced the result." *Per* Middleton, J.A., in *Re Dairy Corp. of Canada Ltd.*, [1934] 3 D.L.R. 347. See also *Garvie v. Axmith* (1961), 31 D.L.R. (2d) 65.

17 All applicable security regulations and stock exchange rules must be strictly complied with.

18 *Re Langley's Ltd.*, [1938] 3 D.L.R. 230; *Montreal Trust Co. v. Oxford Pipe Line Co.*, [1942] 2 D.L.R. 703; aff'd [1942] 3 D.L.R. 619; *Re N. Slater Co. Ltd.*, [1947] 2 D.L.R. 311.

197. Possession of proxies

Proxies, on being deposited, become records of the company.[19] The chairman, scrutineers and all persons entitled to vote may examine the proxies[20] at any reasonable time, during or after the meeting.

> *Comment:* The same rule applies to ballots (Rule 169). Adequate precautions should be taken to prevent any tampering with or disappearance of the proxies so long as the possibility of controversy exists.

WHO MAY APPOINT PROXY

198. Who may appoint proxy

Every person or corporation entitled to vote is entitled to appoint a proxyholder, revoke such appointment and appoint another proxyholder. Under some statutes a corporation may appoint an individual to represent it at meetings.

> *Comment:* Under the new Ontario *Business Corporations Act* (S.O. 1982, c. 4, Section 101) a corporation may by resolution appoint an individual to represent it at meetings.

199. Unregistered holder

Beneficial owners of shares who are not registered are not entitled to appoint proxyholders or to vote, except as provided in the statute.

> *Comment:* The beneficial owner of shares may direct the registered owner to vote as he specifies,[21] and the chairman must accept the vote of, or the appointment of a proxyholder by the registered owner.[22] The chairman has no power to question the right of registered holders to vote or appoint proxyholders or whether or not they are the beneficial owners of the shares.[23] Where both the registered and beneficial owner join in appointing a proxyholder the company cannot reject the vote.[24]

---

19 Rule 169.

20 Proxies must be "accessible to the meeting and open to the inspection of all entitled to vote". (*Spurr v. Albert Mining Co.* (1874), 15 N.B.R. 260.)

21 *Wise v. Landsdell,* [1912] 1 Ch. 420.

22 *Burns v. Siemens Bros. Dynamo Works, Ltd.,* [1919] 1 Ch. 225.

23 *Murphy v. Lindzon,* [1969] 1 O.R. 631; *Pender v. Lushington* (1877), 6 Ch. D. 70; *Tough Oakes Gold Mines Ltd. v. Foster* (1917), 34 D.L.R. 748; *Dominion Royalty Corp. v. Holborn* (1932), 41 O.W.N. 288; *Re Marshall Boston Iron,* unreported S.C.O. motion, October 27, 1981.

24 *Stephenson v. Vokes* (1896), 27 O.R. 691.

200. Nominee holder

A person in whose name shares are registered but who is not the beneficial owner, cannot vote or cause those shares to be voted[25] but, he may, in accordance with instructions from the beneficial owners, issue separate proxies appointing the proxyholder requested by each such beneficial owner and indicate the number of shares to be voted by each proxyholder.

> *Comment:* This situation usually occurs where shares are registered in the name of a stockbroker. He is obligated to send all information and proxy material to the beneficial owner and to vote or give proxies as directed by each respective beneficial owner.

WHO MAY ACT AS PROXYHOLDER

201. Shareholders

In the absence of provisions to the contrary in the governing statute[26] or the constitution, a proxyholder must himself be entitled to vote at the meeting. Where the proxyholder is required to be a shareholder it is sufficient if he becomes one at any time before he votes.[28] Where the shareholder is a corporation it may appoint a representative.[29]

> *Comment:* Where a shareholder is in arrears as to calls, he may nevertheless act as a proxyholder, even though he cannot vote[30]. When a proxyholder, not a shareholder, votes improperly and no objection is taken at the meeting, the validity of such a vote cannot afterwards be disputed.[31]

202. Naming the proxyholder

In the absence of a provision to the contrary in the governing statute[32] or the constitution, the proxyholder need not be specifically named. He may be described by the office he holds or in any other manner.

---

[25] The registrant ought to forward to the beneficial owner, the notice of meeting and accompanying soliciting material immediately on receipt, and request voting instructions. In some provinces the material is to be sent by the company at the registrant's expense. (*Securities Act*, R.S.O. 1980, sec. 48.)

[26] Under most statutes, the proxyholder need not be himself entitled to vote. See relevant statute.

[28] *Bombay-Burmah Trading Corp., Ltd. v. Dorabji Cursetji Shroff*, [1905] A.C. 213.

[29] See Rule 210.

[30] *Colonial Ass'ce Co. v. Smith* (1912), 4 D.L.R. 814.

[31] *Colonial Gold Reef, Ltd., v. Free State Rand, Ltd.*, [1914] 1 Ch. 382.

[32] See footnote 25, *supra* and Rule 217.

Comment: At common law it is not necessary to name the proxyholder specifically. See Rule 217. It is sufficient if he is described, *e.g.,* "The chairman of the meeting"[33] or "A partner in the firm of W. & Co.".[34]

203. Multiple appointees

A shareholder may appoint, on one proxy form, two or more persons as proxyholders. If this is done, the vote on all shares is counted as the majority voted. In case of a tie their joint vote is nullified.[35]

Comment: It is therefore undesirable to appoint an even number of proxyholders to vote the same shares.[36]

204. Multiple documents

A shareholder may execute more than one proxy form appointing different proxyholders on each and fixing the number of shares which each may vote. If the aggregate of the shares does not exceed the total registered in the name of the appointor, their votes are counted. If the aggregate of the shares exceeds the number of shares registered in the name of the appointor, none of the votes shall be counted unless all the proxyholders vote in a like manner.

Comment: See Rules 219-223 for different conditions and instructions on multiple appointments.

FORM OF APPOINTMENT

205. Requirements

Proxy forms must conform with the constitution and applicable corporation and securities acts and regulations. Proxy forms must indicate the creation of an agency by which the

---

33 *Sadgrove v. Bryden,* [1907] 1 Ch. 318.

34 *Bombay-Burmah Trading Corp., Ltd. v. Dorabji Cursetji Shroff, supra; Schmidt v. Mitchell,* 101 Ky. 570 (1897).

35 *Pitt v. Hadrill* (1917), 55 Que. S.C. 166.

36 By giving a proxy to four persons, dividing equally on the choice of a candidate, the shareholder loses his vote through his own fault but such proxy is valid. *Nesbitt, Thompson & Co. Ltd. v. McColl-Frontenac Oil Co. Ltd.* (1938), 43 Que. P.R. 138. In *Re Davey Corp. of Canada Ltd.,* [1934] 3 D.L.R. 347. See Rule 200.

appointee is empowered to exercise the voting rights of the appointor. They need not specify a particular meeting[37] unless required by the statutes or the constitution. They must not contain any material not permissible under the statutes.[38]

206. Contents of proxy form (general)

A proxy form must contain:

(1) The date;[39]

(2) The act of appointment;[40]

(3) The name of the proxyholder;[41]

(4) The signature of the appointor.[42]

It may also contain:

(5) A revocation of any former appointment;[43]

(6) Instructions as to the manner in which the shares covered by the appointment are to be voted;[44]

(7) The number of shares to be voted;[45]

(8) Expiry date of the appointment;[46]

(9) Authority to act at the meeting as the appointor could.

207. Contents of proxy form (special)

Subject to the provisions of the appropriate corporation and securities acts[47] and regulations, if the proxy is solicited, it must contain:

---

[37] *Isaacs v. Chapman* (1915), 32 T.L.R. 183, aff'd 32 T.L.R. 237.

[38] *Re National Grocers Co. Ltd.*, [1938] 3 D.L.R. 106; *Re Langley's Ltd.*, [1938] 3 D.L.R. 230; *Montreal Trust Co. v. Oxford Pipe Line Co.*, [1942] 2 D.L.R. 703, aff'd [1942] 3 D.L.R. 619; *Re Western Canada Flour Mills Ltd.*, [1945] 1 D.L.R. 589; *Re N. Slater Co. Ltd.*, [1947] 2 D.L.R. 311.

[39] Rule 216.

[40] Rule 205.

[41] Rules 202, 217.

[42] Rules 208, 214.

[43] Rules 226, 228.

[44] Rules 219—221.

[45] Rule 227.

[46] Rule 196.

[47] *Murphy v. Lindzon et al.* (1969) 1 D.R. 631.

(1) The date, or a specifically designated blank space for dating the proxy;[48]

(2) The act of appointment;[49]

(3) The name of the proxyholder;[50]

(4) The signature of the appointor;[51]

(5) A statement in bold face type indicating whether or not the proxy is solicited by or on behalf of the management of the company;

(6) Means whereby the appointor is afforded an opportunity to designate a person of his choice as proxyholder;

(7) Means whereby the appointor is afforded an opportunity to specify that the shares shall be voted in favour of or against (in accordance with the choice of the appointor) each matter or groups of related matters intended to be acted upon[52] other than the election of directors and the appointment of auditors, and to specify whether the proxyholder shall have discretionary authority with respect to amendments or variations to the matters not covered in the proxy form or solicitation material.[52]

It may also contain:

(8) A revocation of a former appointment;[53]

(9) Restrictions, limitations or instructions as to the manner in which the shares shall be voted or which may be necessary to comply with the laws of any jurisdiction in which the shares of the company are listed on a stock exchange;[54]

(10) A restriction or limitation as to the number of shares in respect of which the proxy is given;[55]

(11) The meeting for which the proxy has been solicited.[56]

---

[48] Rule 216.

[49] Rule 205.

[50] Rules 202, 217.

[51] Rules 208—214.

[52] *Goldhar et al. and D'Aragon Mines Ltd., Re,* 15 O.R. (2d) 80.

[53] Rules 226—228.

[54] Rules 219—223.

[55] Rule 222.

[56] In some jurisdictions proxies are limited to one meeting. Rules 196, 218.

EXECUTION

208. Signature of appointor

The proxy must be executed by the shareholder or his attorney duly authorized in writing. The signature should conform exactly with the name on the register.[57] The onus is on the proxy-holder to prove the authority of the person signing the document.

> *Comment:* If in doubt, the chairman (or the scrutineers) may verify the signature of the appointor, although there is no obligation on them to do so. The chairman has no authority to question the appointor's rights respecting the shares held by him in trust for the beneficial owner[58] so long as the appointor is the registered holder.

209. Partnership[59]

A proxy given by a partnership must be signed with the name of the partnership.

> *Comment:* Acceptable signatures are "Jones & Co."; "Jones & Co., *per* A. Jones." Where shares were registered in the name of "Roytor & Co. No. 2 Ac." (Roytor & Co. was a partnership formed for the purpose of holding and transferring securities for the account of a chartered bank) a proxy signed "Roytor & Co., No. 2 Ac." is acceptable.[60]

210. Corporation

A corporation which is a shareholder may appoint a proxy-holder,[61] and, if the statute or the constitution so requires, affix its seal thereto.[62] The proxy should be executed by an officer. If executed by an attorney (who is not an officer) it requires a seal or a certified copy of the resolution appointing the attorney.

> *Comment:* A proxy signed with the name of a corporation and the signature of a person describing himself as an officer is *prima facie* evidence of the authority, and the chairman should receive it and permit the appointee to

---

[57] Rules 192, 229.

[58] *Gray v. Yellowknife Gold Mines Ltd.,* [1946] O.W.N. 938; *Murphy v. Lindzon,* [1969] 1 O.R. 631; *Pender v. Lushington* (1877), 6 Ch. D. 70.

[59] See the appropriate Partnership Act.

[60] *Gray v. Yellowknife Gold Mines Ltd., supra;* Rule 229.

[61] *Re Indian Zoedone Co.* (1884), 26 Ch. D. 70.

[62] See Rule 229 (Signatures).

vote.[63] When the document is under seal, the chairman, knowing that the company is a shareholder, should not assume that the seal was illegally affixed or that the person signing as an officer was not authorized to sign.[64]

211. Joint names

When shares are registered in more than one name, with or without right of survivorship, proxies must be signed by all the registered holders unless the governing statute or the articles or bylaws provide otherwise.

> *Comment:* Where the constitution provides that any one of them may in the absence of the others vote on the shares held jointly, a vote by any one of them in person or by proxy, in the absence of a contrary vote by any other of them in person or by proxy is acceptable. See Rule 158.

212. Executors or trustees

Where shares are registered in the names of executors or trustees, proxies must be signed by all of them, unless the articles or bylaws provide otherwise.[65]

213. Association

A proxy given by an association must be signed with the name of the association and the signature of an officer or officers thereof and, if a seal is required under the bylaws of the association, it must be sealed.

214. Attestation

Unless the articles or bylaws require that appointments be attested, attestation is not necessary. If a proxy requires attestation and it is signed with an "X" or other mark, it must be attested and

---

[63] *Re Routley's Holdings Ltd.*, [1959] O.W.N. 89; aff'd 22 D.L.R. (2d) 410, Rule 229.

[64] *Johnson v. Hall* (1957), 10 D.L.R. (2d) 243. Rules 192 and 229.

[65] *Lumbers v. Fretz*, [1928] 4 D.L.R. 269, 854; aff'd [1929] 1 D.L.R. 51.

an affidavit of execution attached, or the signature guaranteed by a
bank or trust company.[66]

> *Comment:* A proxyholder cannot attest his own appointment[67]
> if attestation is necessary.

BLANKS

215. Implied authority

The proxyholder has an implied authority to fill in some
blanks in the proxy. Such blanks must be filled in before the proxy
is deposited with the company.[68]

216. Date omitted

An undated proxy, once deposited, is invalid.

> *Comment:* The date may be filled in under the implied
> authority before the proxy is deposited.

217. Name of proxyholder omitted

A proxy omitting the name of the proxyholder is invalid.

> *Comment:* The name of the proxyholder must be filled in
> before the proxy is deposited.[69] See Rule 202.

218. Date of meeting omitted

If provision is made in the proxy for the date of the meeting[70]
and it is left blank, it may be inserted by the proxyholder or by
any other person duly authorized by the appointor before it is
deposited.

> *Comment:* The date may be inserted after execution if at the
> time of the execution the date of the meeting had not been
> fixed,[71] or if the notice gave the date, but the proxy form
> made no provision for it.[72]

---

66 *Harben v. Phillips* (1882), 23 Ch. D. 14.

67 *Re Parrott; Ex parte Cullen,* [1891] 2 Q.B. 151.

68 *Sadgrove v. Bryden* [1907] 1 Ch. 318.

69 *Re Lancaster* (1877), 5 Ch. D. 911.

70 In some jurisdictions the statutes require the date of the meeting to be
included in the proxy.

71 *Sadgrove v. Bryden,* [1907] 1 Ch. 318.

72 *Ernest v. Loma Gold Mines Ltd.,* [1896] 2 Ch. 572; aff'd [1897] 1 Ch. 1.

RESTRICTIONS AND INSTRUCTIONS

219. Conditions and instructions

In most jurisdictions proxies may contain restrictions, limitations or instructions as to the manner in which the shares held by the appointor are to be voted.

220. Instructions

Proxies may instruct the proxyholder to vote in favour of or against any specific motion. Unless specific authority in the document or the notice permits voting on a modification of the motion, the proxyholder cannot vote on a modified motion.[73]

221. Division of instructions

A shareholder may execute more than one proxy form, each containing different conditions, limitations or instructions.

> *Comment:* When shares arc held by more than one owner or when a nominee holds shares for more than one beneficial owner, one of the owners may in one proxy instruct his proxyholder to vote a specified number of his shares in one way and in another proxy instruct another proxyholder to vote a specified number of his shares in a different way. A proxyholder may be given one proxy directing a specific number of shares to be voted in favour of a proposal and another proxy directing a specific number of shares to be voted against the proposal, or a proxyholder may be appointed in respect of one portion of the shares and another proxyholder appointed in respect of another portion of the shares.

222. Limitation as to number

Proxies may restrict the number of votes which the proxyholder may cast on behalf of the appointor.

223. Conditions carried over from the notice

If the notice or solicitation for proxies or information circular contains any undertaking on the part of the party soliciting the proxy, proxyholders appointed as a result thereof are bound by the terms of the notice or solicitation and must vote in accordance therewith. They cannot vote for any modification or alteration of the resolution unless specifically instructed to do so.[74]

---

[73] *Re Langley's Ltd.*, [1938] 3 D.L.R. 230; *Montreal Trust v. Oxford Pipe Line* [1942] O.R. 490 (C.A.).
[74] *Re Langley's Ltd., supra.*

DEPOSITING PROXIES

224. Time for depositing proxies

Unless the statute[75] or the constitution provides otherwise, proxies may be deposited with the company up to the time of voting.[76] If it is required to deposit the documents at a fixed time prior to the meeting, notice of such a requirement must be given in the notice convening the meeting.

> *Comment:* Where proxies are required to be lodged a certain number of hours before a meeting or adjourned meeting, it is not sufficient to lodge them the specified number of hours before the poll is taken.[77] The notice should not imply that the proxies must be deposited at a certain time unless such restriction has been properly authorized under a valid bylaw or resolution to that effect.[78]

225. Postponing time for depositing

Where the meeting has been or is to be adjourned, the time for depositing proxies may be extended by the same procedure as is required for fixing such time for deposit before the original meeting.[79]

> *Comment:* Since a notice convening a meeting cannot be recalled (Rule 41), the resolution fixing the time for deposit of proxies may be rescinded and a new resolution passed fixing a new time for depositing the documents. Notice of the new time must be given in the same manner as a notice of meeting.[80]

---

[75] See table inside back cover.

[76] *Kelly v. Electrical Construction Co.*, (1907), 16 O.L.R. 232.

[77] *Shaw v. Tati Concessions, Ltd.*, [1913] 1 Ch. 292.

[78] Notices may urge the return of the proxies "without delay", but not that they must be "in the hands of the secretary not later than the hour fixed for holding the meeting" (*Re N. Slater Co. Ltd.*, [1947] 2 D.L.R. 311). See also *Re Brazilian Traction Light & Power Co. Ltd.*, [1947] 4 D.L.R. 736. A clause in the notice to the effect that "proxies must reach the secretary of the company at its office up to 2 p.m. on the day of the meeting or thereafter at the place of the meeting not later than the hour fixed for the meeting" was criticized (*Re Dairy Corp. of Canada Ltd.*, [1934] 3 D.L.R. 347).

[79] Rule 224.

[80] As an adjourned meeting is a continuation of the original meeting, proxies cannot be deposited between the two meetings if they are required to be deposited a certain length of time before the original meeting. (*McLaren v. Thomson*, [1917] 2 Ch. 261; *Scadding v. Lorant* (1851), 3 H.L. Cas. 418.)

REVOCATION

226. Revoking appointment

An appointment of a proxyholder may be revoked by the appointor at any time before the power conferred is exercised[81] even where it appears by its terms to be irrevocable.[82]

> *Comment:* When a shareholder attends and votes, his vote must be accepted to the exclusion of the proxyholder.[83]

227. Formal revocation

An appointment of a proxyholder may be revoked at any time either by a form of revocation or by the subsequent execution of an appointment containing a revocation.[84]

228. Revocation by death

An appointment of a proxyholder is automatically revoked by the death of the appointor, but such revocation is not effective until notice of the death of the appointor reaches the company.

---

[81] *Knight v. Bulkeley* (1858), 27 L. J. Ch. 592.

[82] *Schmidt v. Mitchell*, 101 Ky. 570 (1897). *Nadeau v. Nadeau & Nadeau Ltd.*, 6 N.B.R. (2d) 512.

[83] *Cousins v. International Brick Co., Ltd.*, [1931] 2 Ch. 90. "Where a proxy had not been validly revoked in accordance with the article, the shareholder who had given the proxy was free to attend at the meeting and vote personally; and, when he had done this, the vote tendered by the proxyholder was properly rejected."

[84] See Form 12.

VALIDITY

229. Validity of proxies

The validity of a document appointing a proxyholder is always subject to the governing statutes (corporation and securities) and the constitution. The following table comprises a list of acceptable and non-acceptable proxies. The first two columns set out the situation dealt with, the third column indicates the validity of the document, and the fourth column shows the rule number governing the particular situation where appropriate.

Table of Acceptability of Proxies

GENERALLY

			Rule
Basic rule	Document in proper form, purporting to be signed by the registered shareholder and appearing to be genuine	Acceptable	192
Conflict of laws	In cases of conflict between the laws of place of incorporation, place where meeting held and residence of shareholder	Law of place of incorporation shall govern	11
Telegram or cable	Copy submitted by telegram or cable	Not acceptable	
Blanks	Where blanks are left in the document	Not acceptable, but anyone authorized may fill in blanks prior to depositing	215
Extra words	The words "Duplicate Proxy" or other words or phrases of similar meaning	These words have no significance and are treated as if they did not appear	190
	Other words	Acceptable (except in Quebec)	190
Date	Where date is omitted	Not acceptable (See "Blanks", *supra*)	216
Mutilated	Where document is so mutilated as to cast a doubt on the intention of the appointor	Not acceptable	

			Rule
Multiple	Two or more documents bearing different dates	The one bearing the later date is acceptable	
	Two or more documents bearing the same date	The one appearing to have been signed, mailed or deposited later is acceptable	
Revocation	A revocation in a subsequent proxy or a separate document	Last dated form is acceptable	226

APPOINTEE

Blank	Name of appointee left blank	Not acceptable (See "Blanks", *supra*)	217 202
Multiple appointees	Two or more proxyholders appointed and authorized to act singly, jointly, unanimously or in succession	Acceptable	203

INSTRUCTIONS

Specific	Proxyholder not voting as directed by the appointor	Not acceptable	220
Confusing	Instructions confusing or in doubt	Not acceptable	

RESTRICTIONS

Specific	Proxyholder not complying with the instructions given by the appointor	Not acceptable	219
Confusing	Restrictions confusing or in doubt	Not acceptable	

NUMBER OF SHARES

Comparison with the register	Document specifying number of shares agreeing with register	Acceptable	221
	Number specified exceeds registered number of shares	Acceptable only for the number of shares shown on the register	
	Number specified is less than number of shares registered	Acceptable only for the number of shares shown on the document	
Multiple documents and appointees	Two or more documents appointing different proxyholders fixing the number of shares each may vote	Each acceptable if aggregate does not exceed number of shares on the register	203
		None acceptable if aggregate exceeds number of shares on the register unless all vote the same	

Rule 229—continued

SIGNATURES

(1) *Generally*

Signature of shareholder	Signed in pencil or in ink or manually printed	Acceptable	183
	Facsimile signature	Not acceptable unless properly authorized and evidence of authority filed	
	Rubber stamp signature	Not acceptable unless properly authorized and evidence of authority filed	
Spelling	Slight variations in spelling	Acceptable if phonetically similar	
Titles	Mr., Mrs., Miss, Dr., Jr., Sr. or Roman or Arabic numbers following the name	Acceptable whether capacity added or omitted but not acceptable if it does not agree with the title on the register	
Capacity	Shares registered in name of executor, administrator, trustee, guardian, etc., and document signed with or without the capacity shown	Acceptable whether capacity added or omitted, but not acceptable if incorrect capacity is given	
Initials	Initials instead of full name	Acceptable	
	Full name instead of initials	Acceptable if name conforms with initials	
	One of two or more initials different	Acceptable	
	Addition of extra initial or omission of one initial	Acceptable	
Handwriting	Different handwriting on duplicate documents or revocations	Handwriting should be ignored, whether similar or different (there is a presumption that all signatures are valid)	
	Two or more shareholders with same surname and address, handwriting the same on two different documents	Acceptable	
	Two or more registrations in the same or similar surname and address, and only one document deposited	Acceptable for all shares. Presumed to be same shareholder	

Rule

Address	Address added different from that appearing in register	Acceptable	

(2) *Corporations*

Mode of signing	Name of corporation, one or more signatures, indicating offices held, sealed with corporate seal	Acceptable	210
	Name of corporation, with a signature not identified as an authorized officer	Not acceptable unless sealed or accompanied by resolution of authority under seal	210
	Name of corporation only, no seal, no signature	Not acceptable	210
	Name of corporation affixed by rubber stamp	Not acceptable unless accompanied by evidence of authority	210
	Name of corporation omitted, officer signs his name (even though name of corporation appears elsewhere on the document)	Not acceptable	210

(3) *Associations*

Mode of signing	Name of association and signature of an officer and sealed with association seal, if it has a seal	Acceptable	213
	Name of association and signature of authorized officer, no seal, although association has seal	Not acceptable unless accompanied by resolution or authority, under seal	
	Name of association affixed by rubber stamp	Not acceptable unless accompanied by authority	
	Name of association only, no signature, no seal, although association has seal	Not acceptable	
	Name of association omitted; officer signs his name only and not name of association (even though name of association appears elsewhere on the document)	Not acceptable	

Rule 229—continued

(4) *Partnerships*

Mode of signing	For shares registered in name of "A & B":		
	Signed "A & B"	Acceptable	209
	Signed "A & B *per* A"	Acceptable	
	Signed "A & B *per* B"	Acceptable	
	Signed "A & B *per* D"	Not acceptable unless accompanied by evidence of authority	
	Signed "A & B" *per D*", "Partner"	Not acceptable unless accompanied by evidence of authority	209
	Signed "A for A & B"	Acceptable	
	For shares registered in name of "A & Co.":		
	Signed "A & Co."	Acceptable	
	Signed "A & Co. *per* A"	Acceptable	
	Signed "A & Co. *per* D"	Not acceptable unless accompanied by evidence of authority	
	Signed "D for A & B" "Partner"	Not acceptable unless accompanied by evidence of authority	
	Signed "A for A & Co."	Acceptable	
	Rubber stamp	Not acceptable unless accompanied by evidence of authority	

(5) *Brokers*

Operating as partnership	Same as for partnerships (*supra*)	209
Operating as corporation	Same as for corporations (*supra*)	210

Note: Authority for signatures of officers and partners of brokerage firms are usually on file with the stock exchanges and with trust companies which act as transfer agents and registrars.

Rule

(6) *Miscellaneous Shareholders*

Nominees	Shares registered in name of nominee, proxy signed by nominee	Acceptable	200
	Shares registered in name of nominee together with an account or identifying number, proxy signed by nominee	Acceptable if signature contains same account or identifying number, or none, but not acceptable if it differs	
Banks	Same as corporations and nominees		
More than one share- holder (joint share- holders)	All sign	Acceptable	211
	Less than all sign	Not acceptable unless an agreement to the contrary is on deposit with the company or the constitution permits	211
	One signs and other is present in person	Acceptable if both bal- lots vote similarly	
	All sign and one is present in person	Acceptable if all bal- lots vote similarly	
	Shares registered in names of "A or B"	Deemed to be A *and* B	
With right of survivor- ship	All sign	Acceptable	211
	Less than all sign	Not acceptable unless an agreement to the contrary is on deposit with the company	
	Survivor signs as survivor	Not acceptable unless accompanied by evi- dence of death, *e.g.* letters probate, letters of administration, death certificate, newspaper clippings, etc.	
	One survivor signs as exe- cutor or administrator of his co-owner	Acceptable with proof of appointment	

Rule 229—continued

Rule

Deceased shareholder	Shares registered in name of deceased shareholder	May be voted by executor or administrator either in person or by proxy upon presentation of proof of his appointment	212
		If more than one executor or administrator, all must sign (see "Joint shareholder", *supra*)	
Executors and administrators	Shares registered in name of executors or administrators, and document signed by all	Acceptable	212
	Same, but capacity omitted	Acceptable	
	If not signed by all	Not acceptable	
Guardians	Same as executors		212
Trustees	Same as executors (subject to any agreement or court order to the contrary)		
Receivers	Same as trustees		
Mortgagors	Where shares have been mortgaged or hypothecated but are still registered in shareholder's name, proxy signed by registered shareholder	Acceptable	
	Same — with agreement empowering mortgagees to vote, proxy signed by mortgagee	Acceptable, if accompanied by evidence of authority	

It should be emphasized again that the above is always subject to the provisions of the incorporating document, the constitution and the corporation and securities statutes and regulations.

PART II
COMPANY MEETINGS

CHAPTER XI

MOTIONS AND THEIR PURPOSES

The following Table sets out the motions which may be used to accomplish any required result in the conduct of a meeting. A discussion of the procedure follows.

Purpose	Motion	Rule
Introduce business	Main motion	110
Alter motions	Amend	133
	Divide	119-121
Delay discussion	Point of order	92
	Question of privilege	95
Stop discussion	Vote immediately	148
	Object to consideration	147
	Adjourn discussion	144
	Postpone indefinitely	145
	Refer or refer back	146
	Adjourn the meeting	174-176
Suppress motions	Withdraw motion	128
	Object to consideration	147
	Postpone indefinitely	145
Enforce rights	Point of order	92
Review actions	Rescind resolution	122
	Reconsider resolution	123
Close meeting	Conclude; terminate	173
	Adjourn	174
	Recess	175

The simplest and most direct procedure for accomplishing the purpose of the meeting should be used. Indirect, devious, complicated or "tricky" devices should not be encouraged. The able chairman who is familiar with the rules will recommend a simpler method of accomplishing the desired result if one is available. The chairman is fixed with the responsibility of steering motions through their courses, but not with originating motions or influencing opinions. He can do little to protect all the rights of the minority if the minority is apathetic. Nor can he protect all the rights of the majority if the minority is more vigilant and knowledgeable than the majority.

Introducing business

The business of the meeting is carried on by means of motions which, upon receiving favorable votes, become resolutions. A shareholder wishing the company to do something, to order something to be done or to express an opinion about something, makes his wish known by means of a motion. A main motion originates business, directs or authorizes something to be done, adopts, ratifies, approves, confirms or rejects reports, minutes, acts or things done (Rule 110).

Other motions, subsidiary and incidental, guide the process of arriving at the sense of the meeting. Closing motions end the meeting (Rule 170).

Amending motions

When a motion is first proposed, the phrasing is usually the work of the proposer alone. After some discussion has ensued, it sometimes becomes evident that the wording is not wholly acceptable to the meeting, or that it does not fully represent the wishes of the meeting, or that it is only acceptable in part. To remedy these situations, the motion may be either amended (Rule 133) or divided (Rules 119, 121).

Sometimes a motion may be amended in such a manner as to defeat the motion on the floor by making the entire motion (the original motion with the amendments attached thereto) wholly unacceptable to the meeting. This use of the amendment for this purpose is not salutory but is legally permissible. While a motion to amend may not be merely a negative of the original motion (Rule 129), an amendment may be made that so cripples the intent of the original motion as to make it completely worthless or wholly unacceptable to the meeting.

For example, a motion to retain a business consultant to examine the company's operations becomes worthless if an amendment is appended restricting his fee to $10 a day. (This is known as a crippling amendment.) This motion to amend is in order and must be put to a vote. For procedure, see Rule 134. Of course there is nothing to prevent the moving of a sub-amendment to fix the fee at some more reasonable figure.

Dividing a motion permits its component parts to be considered separately, thereby making it easier to comprehend, and gives the meeting the privilege of accepting or rejecting parts of the original motion. Division may be made voluntarily by the chairman with or without a demand by a shareholder (Rule 119), or by the meeting on a motion (Rule 121). Neither method requires the consent of the mover or seconder of the divided motion.

Delaying discussion

These demands attract the immediate attention of the chairman:

Point of order (Rule 92);

Question of privilege (Rule 95).

They interrupt and delay the discussion until the chairman determines their urgency and deals with them.

Stopping discussion

Discussion on a motion may be stopped and no vote taken at the time, or it may be stopped and a vote taken immediately.

To stop the discussion and force an immediate vote these motions may be made:

Vote immediately or

Close discussion (Rule 148).

To stop the discussion and delay the actual voting, the following motions may be made:

Object to consideration (Rule 147);

Adjourn discussion (Rule 144);

Postpone indefinitely (Rule 145);

Refer or refer back (Rule 146);

Adjourn the meeting (Rules 176-179).

Suppressing motions

Although every shareholder has the right to propose questions for consideration, the meeting has the right to suppress any motion which in its opinion is not desirable.

After discussion has started, or while the mover is in the act of proposing his motion, he may sense the overwhelming opposition of the meeting and voluntarily withdraw his motion with or without the consent of the meeting (Rule 128), or the meeting itself might feel that the motion is inopportune, embarrassing, contentious or unnecessary and may object to consideration of the motion (Rule 147).

To suppress a motion without bringing it to a vote the following motions and demands may be made:

Withdraw motion (Rule 128);

Object to consideration (Rule 147);

Rule motion out of order (Rule 127);

Adjourn discussion (Rule 144);

Postpone indefinitely (Rule 145);

Refer or refer back (Rule 146);

Adjourn meeting (Rules 176-179);

Amend by attaching a crippling amendment (see "Amending motions", *supra*).

Enforcing rights

Every registered holder has the following rights with respect to meetings:

Receive notices (Rule 35);

Appoint proxyholders (Rule 188), revoke (Rule 226) and reappoint proxyholders;

Attend meetings (Rule 8) and be provided with adequate room, comfort and facility to hear and participate in proceedings (Rule 9);

Propose motions and amendments (Rule 115);

Enter into discussions (Rule 142);

Question the chairman and the mover of the motion (Rules 93, 94);

Raise points of order (Rule 92);

Vote on all motions (Rule 156);

Nominate candidates, and to be nominated for office.

Reviewing actions

Sometimes the shareholders, having passed a resolution at the same or previous meeting, wish to reconsider the question for any one of a number of reasons: that the matter was dealt with too hastily, that the meeting was not truly representative of the shareholders, or that conditions have changed. Procedural motions cannot be reviewed.

Methods of reviewing a resolution that has been passed or a motion that has been defeated are:

To rescind the resolution (Rule 124);

To reconsider the resolution (Rule 125);

To reconsider the motion (Rule 125).

However, neither of these methods can be used if the motion sought to be reviewed authorized a payment to be made and the payment has been made, or if it elected or appointed someone to an office and that person was present at the meeting or has been notified of his election or appointment, or if the resolution approved a contract and the other party to the contract was present at the meeting or has been notified of the result of the resolution respecting the contract.

If the proposal to review the resolution takes place at a subsequent meeting, and the resolution that is sought to be reviewed required notice to be given to the shareholders, notice of the proposal to review must be given in the same manner as the notice was given for the original resolution.

Closing meetings

There are three forms of the motion to adjourn:

Motion to conclude (Rule 173)—dissolves the meeting permanently;

Motion to adjourn (Rule 174)—suspends the meeting until it is reconvened on the day fixed by the motion;

Motion to recess (Rule 175)—suspends the meeting for a short period only, as in the case of lunch time, waiting for ballots to be counted, permitting private negotiations to be carried on, allowing shareholders to "cool off", etc.

CHAPTER XII

HOW TO CONDUCT A PROXY CONTEST

Control of the corporation

Since few public companies are controlled by an absolute (over fifty per cent) majority of the voting stock, effective or working control is in the hands of a small group, usually holding only a minority of the voting stock. This working control is only effective as long as the majority of the shareholders remain silent and permit the small controlling group to maintain such control and remain "in". Most shareholders are too apathetic to exert themselves and are content to follow management like sheep. Every so often the "outs" organize themselves into a fighting force, oust the "ins" and install a management representing their policy. The battle for control usually ends up in a proxy contest. In the 1960s such contests reached their zenith in intensity and numbers. Unfortunately the law has not kept pace with the exigencies of proxy contests and we must, therefore, sometimes resort to United States cases and practices, adapting them to our circumstances as best we can. In the United States proxy contests have reached a high degree of specialization.

The privilege of voting by proxy, permitted under the various companies acts, causes decisions to be made by mail which once were made at meetings. At one time a single shareholder with a silver tongue could sway an entire meeting. A Daniel Webster could joust with the most devilish management and come out winning. Now it is all done by letters, circulars and the press.

Those of us who were privileged to know Wm. R. Sweeney (Canada's greatest proxy fighter and meeting manipulator) regret his passing and the consequent loss of the exciting drama of a real live proxy fight. It was he who inspired the need for this book.

What takes place today at meetings is only the culmination of a previously conducted mail campaign. The real battle takes place in the press and the mail box. Much of the old glamour and drama of a meeting is gone. What remains is the counting of the prisoners of war—the proxies.

Vulnerability of management

Any management that is controlled by less than an absolute control is vulnerable. As a result, management must always be vigilant. It should at all times:

— appraise its own strength in voting stock;

— watch transfers of shares for fear that some person or group may be accumulating. Watching the transfer sheets may be of some advantage to insurgents as well as to management;

— have a professional trader study the day-to-day trading. His experience may reveal that the stock is being accumulated for more than just investment purposes. For this purpose he may or should make a study of the daily trading, the number of shares traded and the prices paid, the brokers doing the trading, and other factors;

— conduct its affairs so that it is beyond and above reproach;

— pay meticulous attention to the manner of conducting business;

— conduct meetings of the board and of shareholders in strict compliance with the law.

Management should maintain good relations with shareholders at all times. Correspondence from shareholders should be answered promptly and courteously; if they have complaints they should be cleared up quickly. Shareholders do not like being kept in the dark —periodic reports are a great help. Good news is always welcomed. Even unfavourable news should be disclosed, but it would be wise to time a disclosure of this kind so that it should not create an effect that is undesirable.

Appraisal of strength

In appraising its strength, management should on the one hand take into account its own shares, the shares it controls and the shares belonging to friends. On the other hand, shares of any possible opposition (dissident shareholders and their friends) should be considered, and the possibility of enticing some of the opposition into management's camp.

An unknown factor is frequently the amount of stock held in "street name", that is stock held in the names of brokers or underwriters who no longer have any interest in the stock, the purchasers or current owners having failed, for various reasons, to transfer them into their own names. The purchasers are the beneficial owners but are not registered, and therefore cannot vote.

In most jurisdictions a registrant of shares not beneficially owned by him cannot vote those shares unless he sends to the beneficial owner all the soliciting material and requests instructions how the beneficial owner wishes his shares to be voted. He must vote the shares as requested.

Another difficulty in properly appraising management's strength is the practice of some professional investors of not holding all their stock in their own name. Not infrenquently they transfer a few shares in their own name and hold the bulk of them in "street name" as they wish, for personal reasons, to conceal their identity.

The issues

The usual issues raised by insurgents are:

— inefficient management;

— management's lack of integrity;

— illegal acts by management;

— improvident purchase or sale of assets;

— poor earnings or dividends;

— lack of activity, management-wise or market-wise.

When these issues are raised, care should be taken that an issue is not raised which may boomerang and do more harm than good. Care should also be taken with respect to the laws of libel and slander, the regulations of the stock exchanges and the securities commissions, the articles or bylaws of the company and the corporation and securities statutes.

Planning ahead

The natural tendency of shareholders is to remain loyal to management. However, a dissatisfied shareholder is sometimes able to whip up enough of a storm to gather round him other shareholders for the purpose of ousting management. Proxy contests may on occasion be commenced by shareholders who are not dissatisfied, but who wish to gain control of the company for their own personal reasons. Regardless of motive, not many proxy contests are successful. The insurgents have a difficult task. They must supply their own funds and employ their own organization, whereas management, within certain limits, can use the company's treasury to finance the contest as well as use its facilities and personnel. Management has many advantages and the insurgents have many handicaps. Therefore the decision to undertake a contest against management should be considered very seriously and carefully weighed and analyzed.

The insurgents must make the same kind of appraisal of the strength of their stock position as management must make. They must calculate or estimate the number of shares in their group, the number held by friends and the proportion of the "street stock" they can rely on.

Sometimes the insurgents do not plan to oust management but merely wish to defeat management's attempt to do a specific act which requires the consent of the shareholders. If this act requires a majority of two-thirds (as in the case of special resolutions or bylaws for the sale of assets or alteration of the capital structure) the insurgents need have only one vote more than half the number of shares voted by management to defeat management's aim.

Board of strategy

The conduct of a full-fledged proxy contest instigated by either insurgents or management requires the combined talents of at least five experts; namely: a corporation lawyer, an accountant, a public relations expert, a proxy solicitor, and a specialist in the field in which the company is engaged. A stockbroker or professional trader is sometimes added to the team of experts. However, there have been contests won with the help of only two experts, but this is extremely rare.

The lawyer should be a specialist in corporation and securities law and well versed in the rules and regulations of the exchanges and the securities commissions and, of course, the governing statute. Experience in previous proxy contests is definitely an asset. He should be able to advise on strategy and to anticipate, if at all possible, the legal tactics of the opposing force.

The accountant should be familiar with the problems peculiar to the particular industry in which the company is engaged; he should also be familiar with the regulations of the exchanges and securities commissions.

The security analyst should be accomplished in evaluating securities so that he may properly evaluate the company's securities.

The public relations expert should be familiar with mail and telephone solicitation, and also the use of newspapers or publications which may reach shareholders who cannot be reached by direct mail.

The proxy solicitor contacts the shareholders with a view to persuading them to send in their proxies in support of his client. Experience in the sale of stock, particularly of the type of business of the corporation, is an asset; it may take as much ability and persuasion to obtain a proxy as to sell shares. In the United States proxy soliciting has reached a high degree of specialization as yet unknown in Canada, and some firms are exclusively engaged in this profession.

Cost of the contest

The insurgents must be prepared to expend both money and manpower to achieve their aim. An estimate should be made of the anticipated expenses and these should be liberal, since, invariably, many unforeseen items turn up requiring more money than was originally estimated.

Consideration should be given to the following items of expenses:

(1) Legal expenses. A lawyer will study the ammunition and examine the issues. He will examine all solicitation material of both sides and the proxies received by the insurgents and ensure that everything is in compliance with all the rules and regulations pertaining thereto. The lawyer will assist in the strategy of the solicitation. At the meeting he will challenge management's acts and proceedings and examine management's proxies and the ballots cast with the view of having them disallowed. Litigation, protracted and expensive, sometimes results from solicitations. Injunction proceedings may be instituted either before or after the meeting.

(2) Accountant's fees. An accountant will examine the corporation's books and records, annual statements for a period back, and prepare material to prove or substantiate the charges against management arising out of the finances or out of the books and records of the corporation.

(3) Writing fees—the cost of writing the solicitation material. The entire board of strategy takes a hand in the writing, but it must be edited by an expert with "know-how" in the field.

(4) Printing costs — the cost of preparing and mailing all the solicitation material. Sometimes as many as six sendouts are mailed. This entails a substantial cost.

(5) Fees of public relations experts, if any are retained.

(6) Fees of security analysts, if any are retained.

(7) Fees of professional proxy solicitors, if any are retained.

(8) Office expenses — rent, telephone and overhead; clerical help to receive, tabulate, examine and file all proxies until the meeting.

(9) Travel expenses.

(10) Expenses of watchers at the actual count of the proxies and ballots at the shareholders meeting.

Timing

The timing of the campaign is a most serious matter. Management has an advantage over the insurgents, for it can prepare its solicitation material and notice of the meeting long before the date of the meeting is announced or even fixed.

The insurgents can do little without a shareholders' list. When a contest is imminent, the insurgents would do well to obtain a list of shareholders as early as possible.

Management is in the position of striking the first blow. It can prepare all its solicitation material in advance. The first letter in the mail usually receives the most substantial response. The insurgents do not know the date of the meeting or the nature of management's appeal for proxies. They should therefore:

(1) Obtain the list of shareholders, and

(2) Get a letter in the mail prior to the management letter, but not too far ahead, lest its punch be lost.

Management must, of course, reply. Its reply may contain the following: a discussion of a new policy, an undertaking to send more frequent reports, and a new slate of directors (probably including holders of large blocks of shares) or experts in the field of the company's operations or, if management wants to be more aggressive, its reply may contain a direct attack on the leader of the insurgents, or the committee in charge of the insurgents' campaign, or a reply to the insurgents' letter.

Solicitations

It is the duty of the directors to inform the shareholders of their policy and the reasons why it should be maintained and supported by the shareholders[1] and to give reasons for their re-election.

Directors may, at the expense of the company, send proxy forms (accompanied by stamped return envelopes) for the purpose of securing their re-election.[2] They may use the company's personnel and funds for the purpose of putting their recommendations before the shareholders.

Minority shareholders have no right to solicit proxies at the expense of the company, nor are the directors obliged to put forward the arguments of the dissentient shareholders. Except that under certain statutes, dissenting shareholders (5%) may requisition the board to convene a special meeting of shareholders[3] or have management include their proposal or nominations for directors to be considered at the next annual meeting.[4]

Procedure

Although variations are many, a proxy contest is usually conducted as follows:

The insurgents obtain a copy of the list of shareholders;

The insurgents send out their first mail piece consisting of a solicitation letter, a proxy form (containing a revocation of former proxies) and a self-addressed return envelope, if possible before the formal notice of meeting is sent out by management;

---

1 *Peel v. London & North Western Ry. Co.,* [1907] 1 Ch. 5.

2 *Wilson v. London Midland & Scottish Ry. Co.,* [1940] Ch. 393; *Peel v. London & North Western Ry. Co., supra; Campbell v. Australian Mutual Provident Society* (1908), 77 L.J.P.C. 117; *Studdert v. Grosvenor* (1886), 33 Ch. D. 528.

3 Under Section 104 of the *Business Corporations Act,* S.O. 1982, c. 4, the holders of not less than five per cent of the issued shares of a corporation that carry the right to vote may requisition the directors to call a meeting of shareholders for the purposes stated in the requisition. If the board does not call the meeting, any shareholder who signed the requisition may call the meeting.

4 Under Section 98 of the *Business Corporations Act, S.O.* 1982, c. 4.

Management sends out its formal notice of meeting with a proxy form (containing a revocation of former proxies) (see Forms), a return envelope and the other statutory and stock exchange requirements. If possible, management will enclose a direct reply to the insurgents' letter;

The insurgents reply to management's reply and restate their attack, adding more fuel to it. This mailing should also include another proxy form (containing a revocation of former proxies) (See Forms) and another return envelope. Sometimes a simple revocation of proxy is sent instead of or together with a proxy form. This is particularly useful when management requires a two-third majority to accomplish its aim;

Management and the insurgents carry on the battle as long as time permits with solicitations by mail, telephone and even telegraph.

While both groups are battling away, it is possible for a pirate to appear over the horizon and make away with the booty. It has been known to happen that a third group arises out of the mist, using all the ammunition being thrown by the original battlers and through solicitation by mail, phone and telegraph, obtain both revocations and appointments sufficient to defeat the aim of management and oust them out of control of the board and the company.

Conclusion

After all is said and done, the surest way of winning a proxy contest is to have the greatest (or more than the required) number of votes — either by purchase or by verbal or written agreement with other shareholders. Apart from this, luck is the great factor.

It is well to remember what often happens to "the best laid schemes o' mice an' men" but with "a little bit o' luck" you may not lose.

CHAPTER XIII

FORMS

LIST OF FORMS

LIST OF FORMS—continued

FORM 1

Notice of Annual Meeting

NAME COMPANY LIMITED

NOTICE OF ANNUAL MEETING OF SHAREHOLDERS

TAKE NOTICE that the annual meeting of shareholders of NAME COMPANY LIMITED, will be held at ....
on ...., at ...., for the purpose of

(a) receiving,[1] considering and approving the financial statement for the past fiscal year, together with the auditors' report thereon, and all the transactions reflected thereby;

(b) electing directors;

(c) appointing auditors and authorizing the board of directors to fix their remuneration; and

(d) transacting such other business as may properly come before the meeting.

[Insert Forms 1A to 1F if applicable]

Shareholders who will not be attending the meeting are requested to date, sign and return the accompanying proxy in the envelope provided for that purpose.

[Add if applicable]

An information circular accompanies this notice.

DATED ....

On behalf of the board of directors
A.B., Secretary

1A. Depositing Proxies

[To be inserted in Form 1 if applicable and permitted]

Pursuant to a resolution of the board, proxies must be deposited with the Company not less than forty-eight hours (excluding Saturdays and holidays) preceding the meeting.

1B. Closing Transfer Books

[To be inserted in Form 1 if applicable and permitted]

Pursuant to a resolution of the board, the transfer register will be closed for forty-eight hours (exclusive of Saturdays and holidays) immediately preceding the meeting.

1C. Record Date

Shareholders registered as of *[date]* are entitled to notice of and to vote at the meeting. (The transfer books will not be closed.)

---

[1] If management does not seek the approval of the financial statement, use:
— receiving and considering the financial statement for the past fiscal year, together with the auditors' report thereon.

FORM 1—*continued*

1D. Closing Register

Pursuant to a resolution of the board, the transfer register (and branch transfer register) will be closed for a period of forty-eight hours immediately preceding the meeting.

1E. Bearer Warrants

The holder of a bearer share warrant may attend and vote at the meeting by presenting his share warrant at the meeting, or he may deposit his share warrant with the Company at its head office or with the Company's transfer agent [*name and address*] at least [*five*] days before the meeting date. He will then receive voting certificates entitling him to attend and vote, or certificates of deposit and proxy forms. The warrants will be returned to the depositor after the meeting and adjournments.

1F. Bearer Warrants (alternative)

The holder of a bearer share warrant may attend and vote at the meeting by depositing his share warrant with the chairman of the meeting during the meeting and adjournments thereof.

FORM 2

Notice of Special Meeting

NAME COMPANY LIMITED

NOTICE OF SPECIAL[1] MEETING OF SHAREHOLDERS

TAKE NOTICE that a special meeting of the shareholders of NAME COMPANY LIMITED will be held at ...., on ...., at ...., for the purpose of considering, and if thought fit, confirming with or without such variation or amendment as may be made at the meeting,

(i) a special resolution passed by the board on [*date*], which reads as follows: [*set out resolution in full*],

(ii) a special resolution passed by the board on [*date*], a copy of which is annexed hereto and forms part of this notice,

(iii) a resolution of the board passed on [*date*] for [*indicate purpose of resolution*], and to take such action thereon as may be deemed proper. The said resolution reads as follows: .... [*or*, a copy of the said resolution is annexed hereto and forms part of this notice],

(iv) *or*, Bylaw No. .... authorizing the sale of the assets and undertaking of this Company to ...., on the terms set out in the draft agreement annexed to the said bylaw. A copy of this bylaw and agreement accompany this notice.

[*Insert Forms* 1A *to* 1F, *if applicable*]

Shareholders who will not be attending the meeting are requested to date, sign and return the accompanying proxy in the envelope provided for that purpose.

---

[1] In some jurisdictions this is called a special general meeting.

[*Add if applicable*]

An information circular accompanies this notice.

DATED ....

On behalf of the board of directors
A.B., Secretary.

FORM 3

Notice of Annual and Special Meeting

NAME COMPANY LIMITED

NOTICE OF ANNUAL AND SPECIAL MEETING
OF SHAREHOLDERS

TAKE NOTICE that the annual and special meeting[1] of the shareholders of NAME COMPANY LIMITED will be held at ....
on .... at ....
for the purpose of:

(a) considering and, if thought fit, confirming, with or without such variation or amendment as may be made at the meeting, a Special Resolution passed by the board of directors on the ...., which reads as follows: [*or*, a copy of which is annexed hereto and forms part of this notice:]

(*Add any other purposes from Form 2, above*)

(b) receiving, considering and approving the financial statement for the past fiscal year together with the auditors' report thereon and all the transactions reflected thereby;

(c) electing directors;

(d) appointing auditors and authorizing the directors to fix their remuneration; and

(e) transacting such other business as may properly be brought before the meeting.

{*Insert Forms* 1A *to* 1F *if applicable*]

DATED ....

On behalf of the board of directors
A.B., Secretary.

---

[1] In some jurisdictions this is called a special general meeting.

FORM 4

Notice of Adjourned Meeting

NAME COMPANY LIMITED

NOTICE OF ADJOURNED MEETING OF SHAREHOLDERS

To the Shareholders,

NAME COMPANY LIMITED:

TAKE NOTICE that the annual [*or* special] meeting of shareholders of NAME COMPANY LIMITED convened for . . . . [*date*] has been adjourned to . . . . [*place*] on . . . . [*date*] at . . . . [*time*].

DATED . . . .

By order of the board
A.B., Secretary

FORM 5

Notice of Board Meeting

NAME COMPANY LIMITED

NOTICE OF MEETING OF DIRECTORS

TAKE NOTICE that a meeting of the board of directors of NAME COMPANY LIMITED will be held at . . . . on . . . . , the . . . . day of . . . . at . . . .

DATED . . . .

By order of the president

. . . .

(*Secretary*)

FORM 6

Waiver of Notice of Meeting of Shareholders

NAME COMPANY LIMITED

WAIVER OF NOTICE OF ANNUAL (*or* SPECIAL) MEETING
OF SHAREHOLDERS

I hereby waive notice of the time, place and purpose of an annual (*or* special) meeting of shareholders of NAME COMPANY LIMITED to be held on . . . . at . . . . and do hereby consent to the holding of such meeting.

[*Insert Form 6A, if applicable*]

DATED . . . .

(*Signature*)

6A. Ratify Resolutions

[*To be inserted in Form 6 if applicable*]

And I do hereby agree to ratify all the resolutions passed and the business duly transacted at the annual (*or* special) meeting including . . . . [*specify nature of special business intended to be conducted*].

FORM 7

Waiver of Notice of Meeting of the Board

NAME COMPANY LIMITED

WAIVER OF NOTICE OF MEETING OF THE BOARD

We, the undersigned directors of the Company, hereby waive notice of and consent to the holding of a meeting of the board of directors of the Company at .... [place] on the .... [date] at .... [time] and agree to ratify all the resolutions passed and the business transacted thereat.

DATED ....

FORM 8

Declaration of Service of Notice of Meeting

DECLARATION OF SERVICE OF NOTICE

CANADA .... ⎤
PROVINCE OF .... ⎬ IN THE MATTER OF NAME COMPANY LIMITED AND IN THE MATTER OF THE ANNUAL [or SPECIAL] MEETING OF THE SHAREHOLDERS THEREOF:
COUNTY OF .... ⎦

I, ... of the City of ...., in the County of ...., do solemnly declare:

(1) THAT I am .... of NAME COMPANY LIMITED [or, THAT I am .... of the Trust Company, the Transfer Agent and Registrar of NAME COMPANY LIMITED] and as such have knowledge of the matters herein set out.

(2) THAT I did before the hour of [four] p.m. on [date] mail by first class ordinary mail, postage prepaid, to all registered shareholders of the NAME COMPANY LIMITED, at the address appearing on the share register of the Company at the close of business on the [date], and to the Company's auditors, Messrs. C, A and B, the following documents:

(a) Notice of the Annual [or, Special] Meeting of the shareholders of the said NAME COMPANY LIMITED (marked Annex A hereto);

(b) Information circular (marked Annex B hereto);

(c) Proxy form (marked Annex C hereto);

(d) Annual report for the year ended [date] (marked Annex D hereto);

(e) Return envelope (marked Annex E hereto).

AND I MAKE THIS SOLEMN DECLARATION conscientiously believing the same to be true and knowing that it is of the same force and effect as if made under oath and by virtue of the Canada Evidence Act.

DECLARED before me at the
.... of .... in the
.... of .... this _____
...... day of .... 19....

A commissioner, etc.

FORM 9

Proxy Form (Short)

NAME COMPANY LIMITED

PROXY FORM

The undersigned shareholder of NAME COMPANY LIMITED, hereby appoints .... of ....
as proxyholder of the undersigned to attend, act and vote for and on behalf of the undersigned at the annual [*or* special] meeting of shareholders to be held on the .... (including adjournments thereof) and hereby revokes all proxies previously given.

DATED ....

(Signature)

FORM 10

Proxy Form (Long)

NAME COMPANY LIMITED

PROXY FORM

The undersigned shareholder of NAME COMPANY LIMITED, hereby appoints .... if present, or whom failing ....,
as proxyholder, with power of substitution, to attend, act and vote for and on behalf of the undersigned at the annual [*or* special] meeting of shareholders to be held on the .... (including adjournments thereof) in respect of all matters which may come before the meeting in the same manner as the undersigned could do if personally present thereat, the undersigned hereby agreeing to ratify all which such proxyholder may lawfully do by virtue thereof.

[*Insert Forms* 10A, 10B *if applicable*]

The undersigned hereby revokes all proxies previously given.

[*Insert any applicable form from Form* 10C]

DATED ....

(Signature of Shareholder)

10.A. Limitation as to time

[*To be inserted in Form* 10 *if applicable*]

This proxy shall be valid only for a period of .... months from the date hereof.

10B. Limitation as to Number of Shares

[*To be inserted in Form* 10 *if applicable*]

This proxy is limited to .... shares.

10C. Special Instructions

[*To be inserted in Form* 10 *if applicable*]

1. The said proxyholders are authorized and directed to vote in favour of the confirmation of Bylaw No. . . . . (with or without amendment).

2. The said proxyholders are authorized and directed to vote against confirmation of the special resolution increasing the authorized capital of the Company.

3. The said proxyholders are authorized and directed to vote for the election of . . . . and . . . . and such others, if any, as they in their absolute discretion deem advisable.

    [*In the following examples a choice is given to the appointor who indicates his choice by striking out the inappropriate words or inserting the appropriate words.*]

4. The said proxies are authorized and directed to vote (with or without amendment) for [*or* against] the confirmation of Bylaw No. . . . .

5. The said proxyholders are authorized and directed to vote (with or without amendment) for [*or* against) the confirmation of the special resolution increasing the authorized capital of the Company.

6. The said proxyholders are authorized and directed to vote for the election of . . . . and . . . . as directors.

7. The said proxyholders are hereby restricted from voting for the election of . . . . and . . . . as directors.

FORM 11

Proxy Form (Ontario)

THIS PROXY IS SOLICITED BY THE MANAGEMENT
OF
NAME COMPANY LIMITED

PROXY FORM

The undersigned shareholder of NAME COMPANY LIMITED hereby appoints . . . . if present, or whom failing, ... , as proxyholder to attend, act and vote for and on behalf of the undersigned at the special meeting of shareholders of NAME COMPANY LIMITED to be held on the . . . . day of . . . . , 19. . . . and adjournments thereof; and the undersigned hereby revokes all proxies previously given.

The above-named proxyholders are specifically directed to vote all shares registered in the name of the undersigned as follows:

FORM 11—*continued*

( ) FOR

( ) AGAINST   the approval of

( ) ABSTAIN   (set out details of proposed motion)

    (if no choice is specified, to vote FOR)

    Discretionary authority is conferred on the above-named proxyholder with respect to amendments or variations to matters identified in the notice of meeting and other matters which may properly come before the meeting.

DATED this .... day of ...., 19....

(Signature of Shareholder) (See Notes)

NAME COMPANY LIMITED

NOTES TO PROXY FORM

    The signature(s) must be the same as on the share register. If the shares are registered in more than one name, all holders must sign. If a corporation, the proxy form should be signed by an officer, indicating the office held and its corporate seal affixed. If signed by an attorney authorized to do so, the necessary changes must be made in the form. Such authorization, under seal, or a notarial copy thereof, must accompany the proxy.

    This proxy form is to be read in conjunction with the information circular and the notice of meeting.

    If your address is different from that shown, please advise.

FORM 12

Revocation of Proxy

NAME COMPANY LIMITED

REVOCATION OF PROXY

    The undersigned shareholder of NAME COMPANY LIMITED hereby revokes all other proxies given by the undersigned with respect to the annual [*or* special] meeting of the shareholders of NAME COMPANY LIMITED, to be held on .... 19.... and adjournments thereof (save and except a proxy in favour of ....)[1]

DATED ....

(Signature of Shareholder)

FORM 13

Notice of Revocation of Proxy

To NAME COMPANY LIMITED

and to the Chairman of the Meeting

    TAKE NOTICE that I have revoked the appointment of A.A. as my proxyholder with respect to the annual meeting of shareholders of NAME COMPANY LIMITED to be held on [*date*].

DATED ....

(Signature of Shareholder)

---

[1] For other forms and variations see *O'Brien's Encyclopedia of Forms*, Vol. 5, edited by J. M. Wainberg, Q.C.

FORM 14

Agenda for Annual Meeting (Short Form)

NAME COMPANY LIMITED

AGENDA FOR

Annual Meeting of Shareholders held on [*date*]

1. Chairman	Chairman calls meeting to order.
	Names secretary.
	Names scrutineers, if any.
2. Shareholders	Shareholders are to register their names. Proxies are to be deposited.
3. Notice	[If requested] Secretary reads notice calling meeting and affidavit of mailing.
4. Quorum	Secretary [*or* scrutineers] reports on attendance.
	Chairman declares meeting duly constituted.
5. Minutes	[If requested] Secretary reads minutes of last meeting.
	Chairman asks for errors or omissions. Motion to verify. Discussion and vote. Declares result.
6. Financial Statement	Treasurer tables annual report and financial statement.
	Secretary reads auditor's report.
7. Adopting	Motion to adopt financial statement and approve transactions.
	Discussion and vote.
	Chairman declares result.
8. Election of Directors	Chairman calls for nominations. Motion [*or* declaration] closing nominations.
	If exactly the required number is nominated, chairman declares nominees elected.
	If ballot is required, chairman asks for motion directing secretary to cast a single ballot for the election of those nominated.
	If more than required number is nominated, a poll is taken. Chairman declares result of election.
9. Auditor	Calls for motion to appoint an auditor. Vote is taken. Declares result.
10. Other Business	Asks for further business.
11. Conclusion	Motion to conclude meeting.

FORM 15

Agenda for Annual Meeting (Chairman's Agenda)

NAME COMPANY LIMITED

Annual Meeting of Shareholders held on [*date*]

CHAIRMAN'S AGENDA

FORMALITIES

1. The meeting will now come to order.

Chairman
Secretary
Scrutineers

2. This is the annual meeting of the shareholders of Name Company Limited. Pursuant to the bylaws, I, as president of the company, will act as chairman,[1] Mr. S., secretary of the company, will act as secretary.[2] I appoint Mr. T. and Mr. U. scrutineers.[3]

Registration
Proxies

3. Has everyone registered with the secretary? [*or,* scrutineers?] Have all the proxies been deposited?[4] If not, please do so now.

Notice of
meeting

4. The notice calling this meeting of shareholders[5] was mailed to all the shareholders of record on [*date*]. The declaration as to such mailing is available for inspection by any shareholder. The secretary will annex the declaration to the minutes of this meeting.

Scrutineers'
Report

5. Will the scrutineers please submit their report on attendance. The scrutineers' report[6] follows: [*reads report*]. The chair adopts the scrutineers' report, and declares accordingly.

   [*If the scrutineers are not ready, instruct them to report when ready and proceed, if a quorum is known to be present.*]

6. Notice having been served in accordance with the bylaws, and a quorum being present, I declare that this meeting is duly constituted for the transaction of business.

---

[1] If the chairman is to be elected use Form 15A.

[2] If the secretary is to be appointed see Form 15B.

[3] If the scrutineers are to be appointed by the meeting, use Form 15C.

[4] Omit reference to proxies if they were to be deposited prior to the meeting (Rule 199).

[5] If the meeting is one requisitioned by the shareholders or the court the notice may be read.

[6] If the report is not ready, it may be read later. Substitute
   5A. I am advised that there is a quorum present although the scrutineers' report on attendance in detail may not be ready for some time. In the meantime we will proceed with the business of the meeting.

[7] If the chair does not adopt the scrutineers' report, substitute
   6A. The chair has perused all the proxies [*or,* all the proxies questioned by the scrutineers] and declares the attendance at this meeting to be as follows: [*read*].

MINUTES
OF LAST
MEETING

7. The minutes of the last meeting of shareholders[8] are available for perusal by any shareholder. Unless someone wishes them read, the chair will entertain a motion to take the minutes as read and to verify them.

Motion 1

> "RESOLVED that the minutes of the last annual meeting of shareholders held on [*date*] be taken as read, and be verified and approved."

8. You have heard the motion by: . . . .
. . . .
and seconded by: . . . .
Is there any discussion on the motion? All in favour,[9] please signify by raising your right hand.
Any contrary?
Carried [unanimously].

ANNUAL
REPORT

9. The first item of business is to receive and consider the financial statement for the year ended [*date*] (including the balance sheet and accompanying statements, together with the auditors' report thereon) and the report of the board of directors, all contained in the annual report mailed to the shareholders with the notice of this meeting. There are extra copies available here for anyone wishing one.

10. The secretary will please read the auditors' report.

> [*Secretary reads the auditors' report*].

11. The chair will entertain a motion to adopt the financial statement and the annual report.

Motion 2

> "RESOLVED that the financial statement for the year ended [*date*] (including the balance sheet and accompanying statements, together with the auditors' report thereon) and all the transactions reflected thereby and the report of the board of directors, all contained in the annual report, be approved."

12. You have heard the motion by:
. . . .
and seconded by: . . . .
Is there any discussion on the motion?

---

[8] There is no requirement that the minutes of previous meetings be read or verified.

[9] If a poll is demanded use Form 15D.

FORM 15—*continued*

[*Discussion*]

13. There will be a ballot on this motion.[10] The scrutineers will please distribute the ballots and the secretary will instruct as to their completion.

[*Ballots are distributed*]

Will the scrutineers please collect the ballots and report to the chair as soon as possible. In the meantime the meeting will recess for ten minutes while the ballots are being counted.

[*When the scrutineers have reported*]

14. Order. The meeting will now come to order. The chair has received the scrutineers' report. It reads as follows: [*Chairman reads the report and considers its acceptance.*]

15. The chair accepts the scrutineers' report[11] and declares the motion carried.

ELECTION
OF DIRECTORS

16. The next item of business is the election of directors. Under the provisions of the bylaws, [*five*] directors are to be elected and the meeting is now open for nominations.

Nominations

"I NOMINATE the following as directors
. . . .
. . . .
. . . ."

Are there any more nominations?

17. If there are no further nominations,[12] would someone move that nominations be closed?

Motion 3

"RESOLVED that nominations be closed."

18. You have heard the motion by . . . .
. . . . and
seconded by: . . . .

---

[10] If a poll is not desired, a show of hands may be called for: Substitute:
13A. As there is no further discussion, will all those in favour of the motion, please signify by raising their right hand.
Any contrary?
Carried [unanimously].

[11] If the chairman does not adopt the report of the scrutineers, substitute:
15A. The chair does not adopt the scrutineers' report. The chair has examined all the ballots cast and the proxies on which the count is based and declares the result of the poll as follows:
FOR . . . .
AGAINST . . . .
The chair declares the motion carried [*or* defeated, *as the case may be*].

[12] If only the required number is nominated, the chairman may declare nominations closed without a motion to close. If the bylaw requires elections to be by ballot, use Form 15E. If more than the required number is nominated use Form 15F.

[No discussion on this motion]

All those in favour, please signify in the usual manner.

Any contrary?

Carried [unanimously].

19. I now declare ....
.... elected
directors of the company to hold office until their successors are duly elected or appointed.

AUDITORS

20. It is now in order to appoint auditors.

Motion 4

"Resolved that Messrs. A, B and C, chartered accountants, be appointed auditors of the Company to hold office until the next annual meeting or until their successors are duly appointed, and the board of directors be authorized to fix the auditors' remuneration."

21. You have heard the motion by: ....
.... and
seconded by: ....

[No discussion on this motion]

22. All those in favour,[13] please signify in the usual manner,
Any contrary?
Carried [unanimously]. I declare Messrs.
....
.... appointed auditors.

FURTHER BUSINESS

23. Is there any further business to bring before this meeting?

CONCLUSION

24. As there is no further business, the chair will entertain a motion to conclude.

Motion 5

"Resolved that this meeting be concluded."

25. You have heard the motion by: ....
....
and seconded by: ....
[No discussion]
All in favour?
Against?
Carried. The meeting is now concluded. Thank you.

15A. If the Chairman is to be Elected

A temporary chairman is first appointed informally by the meeting (Rule 64).

---

13 If a poll is demanded use Form 15D.

FORM 15—*continued*

Temporary Chairman: (a) In the absence of the president and the vice-president and with your consent, I will act as temporary chairman and conduct an election for the permanent chairman of the meeting.

             (b) The meeting is now open for nominations for chairman.

                         [Nominations are made]

             (c) Are there any further nominations?

             (d) As only one person[14] has been nominated may I have a motion to declare Mr. C elected chairman of the meeting?[15]

             (e) Moved by Mr. M., seconded by Mr. N., that Mr. C., be elected chairman of this meeting.

                 All those in favour please signify in the usual manner by raising the right hand.

                 Contrary, if any?

                 Carried [unanimously]. I declare Mr. C. elected chairman of this meeting.

             (f) I will now retire. Will Mr. C. please take the chair?

15B. If a Secretary is to be Appointed

             (a) The meeting is now open for a motion to appoint a secretary.

             (b) It has been moved by Mr. M., seconded by Mr. N., that Mr. S. be appointed secretary of this meeting.

             (c) All those in favour please signify in the usual manner by raising the right hand.
Contrary, if any?

             (d) Carried [unanimously].[16]

15C. If the Scrutineers are to be Appointed by the Meeting

             (a) Would the meeting like to appoint scrutineers? The chair will receive a motion to that effect.

Motion   "RESOLVED that Mr. T. and Mr. U. be appointed scrutineers."

             (b) It has been moved by Mr. M., seconded by Mr. N., that Mr. T. and Mr. U. be appointed scrutineers of the meeting.

---

[14] If more than one is nominated and a poll is demanded use Form 15D.

[15] Or he may be declared elected by acclamation.

[16] If the motion is defeated, substitute:
    (d) The motion is defeated, may I have another motion to appoint? *[Proceed with* (a), (b) *and* (c) *until a motion is carried successfully appointing a secretary.]*

(c) All those in favour please signify in the usual manner by raising the right hand. Contrary, if any?

(d) Carried [unanimously].[17]

15D. If a Poll is Demanded or Required

(a) As a poll has been demanded [or, is required] the scrutineers will please distribute ballots and the secretary will give instructions in the use of the ballots.

> (*Secretary:* If you are in favour of the motion mark an "X" in the box opposite the word "FOR". If you are against the motion mark an "X" in the box opposite the word "AGAINST". Then sign your name clearly. If you are a proxyholder for absent shareholders indicate clearly how you are instructed to vote the shares of the holders whom you represent.)

(b) Will the scrutineers now collect the ballots?

(c) Are all the ballots in the hands of the scrutineers? If so, the scrutineers will now retire to count the ballots and report back to the chair.

> [*The scrutineers retire and count the ballots. As soon as they are ready they report to the chair in writing on Form 24 or 25. The meeting may be recessed or adjourned while the scrutineers are counting the ballots. When the scrutineers have reported, proceed with the meeting.*]

(d) Order. The meeting will now come to order. The chair has received the scrutineers' report. It reads as follows: [*The chairman reads the report and considers its acceptance.*]

(e) The chair adopts the report of the scrutineers and declares the motion carried [or defeated, *as the case may be.*[18,19]]

---

[17] If the motion is defeated, substitute:
(d) The motion is defeated. May I have another motion to appoint? [*Proceed with* (a), (b) *and* (c) *until a motion is carried successfully appointing scrutineers.*]

[18] If the chairman does not adopt the report of the scrutineers, substitute:
(e) The chair does not adopt the scrutineers' report. The chair has examined all the ballots cast and the proxies on which the count is based and declares the result of the poll as follows:
FOR ....
AGAINST ....
The chair declares the motion carried [or defeated, *as the case may be*].

[19] For other forms and variations of forms, see *O'Briens Encyclopedia of Forms* Vol. 5, edited by J. M. Wainberg, Q.C.

FORM 15—*continued*

15E. If Directors are to be Elected by Ballot

(a) As the bylaws require that the election of directors be by ballot, the chair will receive a motion directing the secretary to cast a single ballot for the election of the persons nominated.

Motion

"RESOLVED that the Secretary be directed to cast a single ballot on behalf of those present at the meeting for the election of the persons nominated as directors."

(b) You have heard the motion by: . . . .
. . . . and
seconded by: . . . .

[*No discussion on this motion*]

All in favour signify in the usual manner.
Any against?
Carried [unanimously].

(c) Will the secretary please cast a ballot as directed.

[*Secretary prepares and casts ballot.*]

(d) I declare . . . .
elected directors of the Company by ballot, to hold office until their successors are duly elected or appointed.

15F. Election of Directors Contested

(a) Are there any further nominations? Will some one move that nominations be closed?

"RESOLVED that nominations be closed."

(b) You have heard the motion by: . . . .
. . . . and
seconded by: . . . .

All in favour indicate by raising the right hand.
Any against?
Carried [unanimously].

(c) The following have been nominated: Mr. A, B, C, E, F and G.

(d) The scrutineers will distribute ballots and the secretary will give instructions for the use of the ballots.

(*Secretary:* "You will mark an "X" opposite the names of the persons of your

---

[20] If the ballots do not contain the names of all the candidates, substitute: (*Secretary:* "You will print on the ballot the names of the persons for whose election you wish to vote. Only persons who have been nominated and whose names have been read by the chair may be voted for. The names of not more than [5] are to be inserted in the ballot. Be sure to sign your name clearly at the foot of the ballot and indicate whether you are casting all your votes as proxy in the same manner.")

choice.[20] You may vote for less than the required number but not for more. You need not vote for the entire slate of candidates of one group. Sign your name clearly and indicate whether you are casting all your votes as proxy in the same manner.")

(e) Will the scrutineers now collect the ballots?

(f) Are all the ballots in the hands of the scrutineers? If so, the scrutineers will now retire to count the ballots and report back to the chair.

> [*The scrutineers retire and count the ballots. As soon as they are ready they report to the chair in writing as in Forms 26 or 27. The chair may recess or adjourn the meeting while the scrutineers are counting the ballots. On receipt of the report, proceed with the meeting.*]

(g) The meeting will now come to order. The chair has received the scrutineers' report which reads as follows:

[reads report]

(h) The chair adopts the report of the scrutineers[21] and declares .... duly elected directors of the company to hold office until their successors are duly elected or appointed.

FORM 16
Agenda for Special Meeting (Short Form)

NAME COMPANY LIMITED

Special Meeting of Shareholders held on ....

AGENDA

1. Chairman	Chairman calls meeting to order.
	Names secretary.
	Names scrutineers, if any.
2. Shareholders	Shareholders are to register their names. Proxies are to be deposited.

---

21 If the chairman does not adopt the report of the scrutineers, substitute:
(h) The chair does not adopt the scrutineers' report. The chair has examined all the ballots and the proxies on which the count is based and declares the result of the balloting as follows:

AB ....
CD ....
DE ....
FG ....
HI ....

The chair therefore declares .... to be duly elected directors of the company to hold office until their successors are duly elected or appointed.

FORM 16—*continued*

3. Notice	[If requested] Secretary reads notice calling meeting and affidavit of mailing.
4. Quorum	Secretary [*or* scrutineers] reports on attendance. Chairman declares meeting duly constituted.
5. Minutes	[If requested] Secretary reads minutes of last meeting. Chairman asks for errors or omissions. Motion to verify. Discussion and vote. Declares result.
6. Special Business	Introduces special business of the meeting. Motion, discussion, vote. Declares result.
7. Conclusion	Motion to conclude.

FORM 17

Agenda for Special Meeting (Chairman's Agenda)

NAME COMPANY LIMITED

Special Meeting of Shareholders held on . . . .

CHAIRMAN'S AGENDA

FORMALITIES

1. The meeting will now come to order.

Chairman
Secretary
Scrutineers

2. This is a general meeting of the shareholders of Name Company Limited. Pursuant to the bylaws, I, as president of the company, will act as chairman,[1] Mr. S., secretary of the company, will act as secretary.[2] I appoint Mr. T. and Mr. U. scrutineers.[3]

Registration

3. Has everyone registered with the secretary? [*or* scrutineers?] Have all the proxies been deposited?[4] If not, please do so now.

Notice of
Meeting

4. The notice calling this meeting[5] of shareholders was mailed to all the shareholders of record on [*date*]. The declaration as to such mailing is available for inspection by any shareholder. The secretary will append the declaration as a schedule to the minutes of this meeting.

---

[1] If the chairman is to be elected use Form 15A.

[2] If the secretary is to be appointed see Form 15B.

[3] If the scrutineers are to be appointed by the meeting, use Form 15C.

[4] Omit reference to proxies if they were to be deposited prior to the meeting (Rule 199).

[5] If the meeting is one requisitioned by the shareholders or the court, the notice ought to be read.

Scrutineers'
Report

5. Will the scrutineers please submit their report on attendance. The scrutineers' report[6] as follows: [*read report*]. The chair adopts the scrutineers' report[7] and declares accordingly.

> [*If the scrutineers are not ready, instruct them to report when ready and proceed if a quorum is known to be present*].

6. Notice having been served in accordance with the bylaws and a quorum being present, I declare that this meeting is duly constituted for the transaction of business.

MINUTES
OF LAST
MEETING

7. The minutes of the last meeting of shareholders[8] are available for perusal by any shareholder. Unless someone wishes them read, the chair will entertain a motion to take the minutes as read and verify them.

Motion 1

> "RESOLVED that the minutes of the last annual meeting of shareholders held on [*date*] be taken as read, and be verified and approved."

8. You have heard the motion by: . . . . and seconded by: . . . .

> Is there any discussion on the motion? All in favour, please signify by raising your right hand.[9]

> Any contrary?

> Carried [unanimously].

SPECIAL
BUSINESS

9. The special business for which the meeting was called is . . . .

> [*Introduces special business*]

> The resolution which was passed by the board on [*date*] is set out in full in the information circular. It requires a two-thirds majority to confirm it. The chair will receive a motion to confirm the special resolution and then we can discuss it.

---

6 If the report is not ready, it may be read later. Substitute:
  5A. I am advised that there is a quorum present although the scrutineers' report on attendance in detail may not be ready for some time. In the meantime we will proceed with the business of the meeting.

7 If the chairman does not adopt the scrutineers' report, substitute:
  6A. The chair has perused all the proxies [*or*, all the proxies questioned by the scrutineers] and declares the attendance at this meeting to be as follows: [*read*].

8 There is no requirement that the minutes of previous meetings be read or verified.

9 If a poll is demanded use Form 15D.

FORM 17—*continued*

Motion 2

"RESOLVED that Special Resolution No. 3 passed by the board of directors on [*date*] as presented to the meeting be confirmed."

Is there any discussion on the motion?

[*Discussion*]

10. As this motion requires a two-thirds majority we will proceed to take the vote by ballot. The scrutineers will please distribute the ballots and the secretary will instruct you as to their completion.

[*Ballots are distributed*]

Will the scrutineers please collect the ballots and report to the chair as soon as possible. The meeting will recess for ten minutes while the ballots are being counted.

[*When the scrutineers have reported*]

The meeting will now come to order. The chair has received the scrutineers' report. It reads as follows: [*reads report*].

11. The chair adopts the scrutineers' report[10] and declares the motion carried by more than a two-thirds majority.

CONCLUSION

12. As there is no further business, the chair will entertain a motion to conclude.

Motion 3

"RESOLVED that this meeting be concluded."

13. You have heard the motion by: . . . . and seconded by . . . . [*no discussion*]

All in favour?

Against?

Carried. The meeting is now concluded.

Thank you.

---

[10] If the chairman does not adopt the report of the scrutineers, substitute:
11. The chair does not adopt the scrutineers' report. The chair has examined all the ballots cast (and the proxies on which the count is based) and declares the result of the poll as follows:

   FOR: . . . .

   AGAINST: . . . .

The chair declares the motion carried [*or* defeated, *as the case may be*].

FORM 18

Agenda for Board Meeting

NAME COMPANY LIMITED

AGENDA

for

Meeting of the board held ....

1. Formalities	Chairman calls meeting to order.
2. Notice	Secretary proves service of notice.
3. Quorum	If quorum present, declares meeting duly constituted.
4. Minutes	Secretary reads minutes of last meeting.
	Chairman asks for errors or omissions.
	Motion to verify.
	Discussion and vote.
	Declares result.
5. Business	Business arising out of minutes.
6. Reports	Reports of officers and committees.
7. Other Business	Asks for further business.
8. Conclusion	Motion to conclude.

FORM 19

Ballot on Motion (Short Form)

NAME COMPANY LIMITED

Ballot on Motion to etc.

I hereby vote all my shares
and all shares represented by me   FOR   ( )
as proxyholder   AGAINST   ( )

....

(Signature of person voting)

FORM 20

Ballot on Motion (Long Form)

NAME COMPANY LIMITED

Ballot on Motion to etc.

General Meeting of Shareholders held on . . . .

I hereby vote all shares registered in my name	For	( )
	Against	( )
I hereby vote all shares represented by me as proxyholder	For	( )
	Against	( )

. . . .
(Signature of person voting)

[*To be filled in by scrutineers*]

Registered holder of . . . . shares

Representing by proxy . . . . shares

NUMBER OF SHARES VOTED . . . .

FORM 21

Ballot on Election of Directors

NAME COMPANY LIMITED

Annual Meeting of Shareholders held on . . . .

BALLOT FOR ELECTION OF DIRECTORS

I vote for the election of:

1. . . . .
2. . . . .
3. . . . .
4. . . . .
5. . . . .
6. . . . .
7. . . . .

This ballot is cast in respect of all shares registered in my name and in respect of all shares registered in the name of each shareholder who has appointed me proxyholder and authorized me to vote thereon.

. . . .
(Signature of person voting)

[*To be filled in by scrutineers*]

Registered holder of . . . . shares

Representing by proxy . . . . shares

NUMBER OF SHARES VOTED . . . .

FORM 22

Scrutineers' Report on Attendance (Short Form)

NAME COMPANY LIMITED

Meeting of Shareholders held on ....

SCRUTINEERS' REPORT ON ATTENDANCE

PRESENT IN PERSON

...... shareholders (as per exhibit A hereto) holding .... shares

REPRESENTED BY PROXY

According to proxies filed in favour of:

.... for .... shares
.... for .... shares
.... for .... shares

Represented by proxy .... shares

TOTAL in person and by proxy .... shares

In addition to the proxies referred to above there are proxies (as per exhibit B hereto) which are, in our opinion, unacceptable and we recommend that they be rejected.

The shares represented in person and by proxy have been checked by us against the shareholders' list furnished by the Company's transfer agent.

DATED ....

....
(Scrutineer)
....
(Scrutineer)

FORM 23

Scrutineers' Report on Attendance (Long Form)

NAME COMPANY LIMITED

Meeting of Shareholders held on ....

PRESENT IN PERSON

.... shareholders holding .... shares

PROXIES FILED in favour of:

		(Name)	*(Name)*	*(Name)*
Motion	Authorized to vote FOR:	....	....	....
No. 1.	AGAINST:	....	....	....
Motion	Authorized to vote FOR:	....	....	....
No. 2.	AGAINST:	....	....	....
Motion	Authorized to vote FOR:	....	....	....
No. 3	AGAINST:	....	....	....

FORM 23—*continued*

PROXIES NOT COUNTED:

Date incomplete ....

Duplicated, later date ....

Duplicated, same date ....

Signed by only one joint holder ....

No corporate seal ....

Not on shareholders' list ....

Otherwise unacceptable ....

TOTAL REJECTED FOR: ....

TOTAL REJECTED AGAINST: ....

These proxies, in our opinion, are unacceptable and we recommend that they be rejected.

The shares represented in person and by proxy have been checked by us against the shareholders' register.

....
(Scrutineer)

DATED ....
(Scrutineer)

FORM 24

Scrutineers' Report on Motion (Short Form)

NAME COMPANY LIMITED

Meeting of Shareholders held on ....

SCRUTINEERS' REPORT ON MOTION TO ....

We, the undersigned scrutineers, report on the balloting on this motion as follows:

FOR THE MOTION   Shares
    In person   ....
    By proxy   ....

                    Total FOR _____

AGAINST THE MOTION
    In person   ....
    By proxy   ....

              Total AGAINST _____

Total votes cast .... shares.

....
    (Scrutineer)   *(Scrutineer)*

FORM 25

Scrutineers' Report on Motion (Long Form)

NAME COMPANY LIMITED

SCRUTINEERS' REPORT ON MOTION No. 1 [*or*, Motion to ....]

We, the undersigned scrutineers, report on the balloting on this motion as follows:

FOR THE MOTION	*Acceptable*	*Not Acceptable*
In person	....	....
By proxy (name of proxy)	....	....
(name of proxy)	....	....
(name of proxy)	....	....
TOTAL FOR		

AGAINST THE MOTION		
in person	....	....
By proxy (name of proxy)	....	....
(name of proxy)	....	....
(name of proxy)	....	....
TOTAL AGAINST		

The ballots not counted were set aside in accordance with the chairman's declaration as to the acceptability of the respective proxies:

DEFECT:	IN FAVOUR OF		
	(Name A.)	*(Name B.)*	*(Name C.)*
Proxy not dated	....	....	....
Duplicated, later dated	....	....	....
Duplicated, same date	....	....	....
Signed by only one joint holder	....	....	....
No corporate seal	....	....	....
Not on shareholders' list	....	....	....
Otherwise unacceptable	....	....	....

The shares represented in person and by proxy have been checked by us against the shareholders' register [*or*, shareholders' list dated ....]

....
(*Scrutineer*)

DATED ....
(*Scrutineer*)

FORM 26

Scruitneers' Report on Election of Directors (Short Form)

NAME COMPANY LIMITED

SCRUTINEER'S REPORT ON ELECTION OF
DIRECTORS

[*Date*]

Candidates	*Votes*
1.	....
2.	....
3.	....
4.	....
5.	....
6.	....
7.	....

....
(*Scrutineer*)   (*Scrutineer*)

FORM 27

Scruitneers' Report on Election of Directors (Long Form)

NAME COMPANY LIMITED

SCRUTINEERS' REPORT ON ELECTION OF
DIRECTORS

We, the undersigned scrutineers, report on the balloting on the election of directors as follows:

Candidates	*Votes Allowed*	*Disallowed*
1.	....	....
2.	....	....
3.	....	....
4.	....	....
5.	....	....
6.	....	....
7.	....	....

The disallowed votes are based upon proxies which were disallowed by the chairman.

In addition and not counted were .... ballots which in our opinion are defective because:

too many candidates	....
signature indecipherable	....
other defects	....

....
(*Scrutineer*)

DATED ....
(*Scrutineer*)

FORM 28 ı

Minutes of Annual Meeting (Public Company)

MINUTES of the annual meeting of shareholders of NAME COMPANY LIMITED, held at .... [*place*] on .... [*date*] at ....[*time*].

Formalities

Mr. C., the president of the Company, called the meeting to order and acted as chairman of the meeting, and Mr. S., secretary of the Company, acted as secretary of the meeting.[1] The chairman appointed Mr. T. and Mr. U. scrutineers.[2]

Notice of meeting

Notice calling this meeting of shareholders[3] was sent to all registered shareholders of the Company on [*date*] in accordance with the bylaws [*or* articles] of the Company, as evidenced by the declaration of Mr. ...., Clerk of the Stock Transfer Department of the Trust Company, Registrar and Transfer Agent of the Company. The declaration is annexed to these minutes as Annex "A".

Attendance

The scrutineers reported that there were (   ) shareholders present in person holding (   ) shares, and there were (   ) shares represented by proxy, of which (   ) were in favour of M.C. and (   ) shares in favour of W.A. The chairman adopted the report of the scrutineers and declared accordingly. The Scrutineers' Report on Attendance is annexed to these minutes as Annex "B".

Constitution of meeting

The chairman declared that notice of this meeting had been duly given to all registered shareholders of the Company in accordance with the bylaws [*or,* articles] of the Company, that there was a quorum present, and that the meeting was duly constituted for the transaction of business.

Minutes of last meeting

The chairman advised the meeting that the minutes of the last meeting of shareholders[4] were available for perusal by the shareholders and would be read if any shareholder so desired.[5] No shareholder made such a request, and upon motion duly made by Mr. L., seconded by Mr. M. and unanimously carried, it was

RESOLVED that the minutes of the annual meeting of the shareholders held on the [*date*] be taken as read and verified.

---

1 For variations, see Form 28A.

2 For variations, see Form 28B.

3 For variations, see Form 28C.

4 Unless required by the articles or the bylaws, reading or verifying the minutes of previous meetings is not necessary.

5 For variations, see Form 28E.

FORM 28—*continued*

Annual report

The chairman presented to the meeting the financial statement for the year ended [*date*] (including the balance sheet and accompanying statements, together with the auditors' report thereon) and the report of the board of directors, all contained in the annual report. The secretary read to the meeting the auditor's report for the year ended [*date*]. The following motion was made by Mr. G. and seconded by Mr. H.:

RESOLVED that the financial statement for the year ended [*date*] (including the balance sheet and accompanying statements, together with the auditor's report thereon) and all the transactions reflected thereby and the report of the board of directors, all contained in the annual report, be approved.

A poll was taken and the chairman declared the resolution duly CARRIED by a vote of (   ) votes FOR and (   ) votes AGAINST. The Srutineers' Report is annexed to these minutes as Annex "C".

Election of directors

The chairman called for nominations for directors of the Company and the following persons were nominated:

Upon motion duly made, seconded and unanimously carried, nominations were closed.[6]

Only five persons having been nominated and no shareholder having demanded a ballot,[7] the chairman declared . . . . to be duly elected directors of the Company to hold office until their successors are duly elected or appointed.

Appointment of auditors

Upon motion duly made by Mr. P. and seconded by Mr. Q. and unanimously carried, it was

RESOLVED that Messrs. . . . . be appointed auditors of the Company to hold office until the next annual meeting or until their successors are duly appointed, and the board of directors be authorized to fix the remuneration of the auditors. [*Add if indicated:* on the basis of that presently paid.]

Conclusion

Upon motion duly made by Mr. M. seconded by Mr. N. and unanimously carried, the meeting was concluded.

. . . .
        (Chairman)   *(Secretary)*

VERIFIED at the meeting of shareholders held . . . .

. . . .
                       (Chairman)

---

[6] For variations, see Form 28F.

[7] For variations, see Form 28F.

28A. Variations—Chairman and Secretary

(i) *If the vice-president chaired the meeting*

In the absence [*or* refusal] of the president, Mr. D., the vice-president, acted as chairman of the meeting.

(ii) *If the chairman was elected by resolution*

On motion duly made by Mr. M., seconded by Mr. N. and unanimously carried it was

RESOLVED that Mr. C. be elected chairman of the meeting. Mr. C. acted as chairman.

(iii) *If the chairman was elected by ballot*

Mr. C. and Mr. D. were nominated for chairman of the meeting. A poll was taken, and Mr. C. was declared elected and acted as chairman of the meeting.

(iv) *If the chairman and secretary were elected by resolution*

On motion duly made by Mr. M., seconded by Mr. N. and unanimously carried it was

RESOLVED that Mr. C. be elected chairman and Mr. S. be appointed secretary of the meeting.

(v) *If the secretary was appointed by resolution*

On motion duly made by Mr. M., seconded by Mr. N. and unanimously carried it was

RESOLVED that Mr. S. be and he is hereby appointed secretary of the meeting.

28B. Variation—Scrutineers

On motion duly made, seconded and unanimously carried it was

RESOLVED that Mr. T. and Mr. V. are hereby appointed scrutineers to assist the chairman in counting attendance, proxies and ballots.

28C. Variation—Notice Mailed

The chairman declared that notice of this meeting having been mailed to each shareholder in accordance with the bylaws [*or* articles] of the company, and a quorum being present, the meeting was duly constituted for the transaction of business.

28D. Variation—If the Report on Attendance was not Ready

The chairman stated that the report on attendance was not ready. He declared that there was a quorum present and that the meeting was duly constituted for the transaction of business. Subsequently the scrutineers' report on attendance was submitted and the chairman adopted the report and declared the attendance at the meeting to be as follows:

Present in person .... shareholders holding .... shares

Represented by proxy in favour of ...., ... shares

Represented by proxy in favour of ...., ... shares

The scrutineers' report was directed to be annexed to the minutes of the meeting and the proxies filed with the records of the Company.

FORM 28—*continued*

28E. Variation—If Minutes Taken as Read

Upon motion duly made, seconded and unanimously carried, it was

RESOLVED that the minutes of the previous meeting of shareholders held on .... be taken as read and verified.

28F. Variations—Election by Acclamation

(i) *Nominations closed by resolution*

The chairman called for further nominations and none were offered. On motion duly made, seconded and unanimously carried it was

RESOLVED that nominations be closed.

(ii) *Nominations. Election by ballot*

The chairman called for further nominations. None were offered and the chairman declared nominations closed.[8] Upon motion duly made by Mr. M., seconded by Mr. N., and unanimously carried, it was

RESOLVED that only five persons having been nominated as directors of the Company, and the chairman having declared nominations closed, the secretary be directed to cast a single ballot for the election of those nominated as directors.

The secretary cast a ballot as directed and the chairman thereupon declared .... to be duly elected directors of the Company to hold office until their successors are duly elected or appointed.[8]

FORM 29

Minutes of Annual Meeting (Private Company)

MINUTES of the annual meeting of shareholders of NAME COMPANY LIMITED, held at .... on .... at .... PRESENT [*set out names*] being all [*or* a quorum] of the shareholders of the Company.

Formalities

Mr. C., president of the Company, acted as chairman of the meeting and Mr. S., secretary of the Company, acted as secretary of the meeting.[1]

The chairman declared that all the shareholders being present in person and having waived notice calling this meeting, the meeting was duly constituted for the transaction of business.[2]

Minutes of last meeting

The minutes of the meeting of shareholders[3] held .... were read by the secretary, and, on motion duly made, seconded and unanimously carried, it was

---

8 For other variations, see Form 30.

1 For variations see Form 28A, *supra*.

2 For variations, see Form 28C, *supra*.

3 Unless required by the articles or bylaws, reading or verifying the minutes of previous meetings is not necessary. Omit if previous minutes have been verified by signing.

RESOLVED that the minutes of the meeting of shareholders held . . . . .
. . . . be verified.

[*If minutes of previous meeting were taken as read use Form* 28E.]

Financial statement

The chairman then submitted the financial statement for the year
ended [*date*] including the balance sheet and related statements. The secretary read the auditor's report to the meeting.

On motion duly made, seconded and unanimously carried, it was

RESOLVED that the financial statement for the year ended [*date*] including the balance sheet and related statements and auditor's report for the
year ended [*date*] be approved.

Acts of directors

On motion duly made, seconded and unanimously carried, it was

RESOLVED that all the acts, proceedings, contracts, bylaws, appointments, elections and payments, enacted, made, done and taken by the
board of directors and the officers of the Company since the last annual
meeting of shareholders as recorded in the minutes of meetings of the
board and the shareholders or on the books or records of the Company,
be approved and ratified.

Election of directors

The chairman called for nominations for directors of the Company
and the following persons were nominated . . . .
There being no further nominations and no shareholder having demanded
a ballot, and on motion duly made, seconded and unanimously carried,
it was

RESOLVED that [*set out names*] are elected directors of the Company
to hold office until their successors are duly elected or appointed.[4]

Appointment of auditors

On motion duly made, seconded and unanimously carried, it was

RESOLVED that C.A. & Co. be appointed auditors of the Company, to
hold office until the next annual meeting of shareholders or until their
successors are duly appointed, at a remuneration to be fixed by the board,
the board being authorized to fix such remuneration on the basis of that
presently paid.[5]

Conclusion of meeting

There being no further business, the meeting was concluded.

. . . .
        (Chairman)   *(Secretary)*

---

[4] If a poll by ballot is required under the articles or bylaws, use the
second and third paragraphs under "Election of Directors" in Form 28.

[5] For variation use the section "Annual Report" in Form 28, *supra.*

FORM 29—*continued*

We, the undersigned, verify the above minutes and acknowledge having waived notice of the meeting. We approve all the resolutions passed and business transacted thereat.

. . . .

. . . .

. . . .

[*If the minutes are verified at a subsequent meeting, use the following in place of the above waiver*]

VERIFIED at meeting of shareholders held on . . . .

. . . .

(*Chairman*)

FORM 30

Minutes of Annual Meeting (Business Contested)

MINUTES of the annual meeting of shareholders of NAME COMPANY LIMITED, held at . . . . [*place*] on . . . . [*date*] at . . . . [*time*].

Formalities

Mr. C., the president of the Company, called the meeting to order and acted as chairman of the meeting, and Mr. S., secretary of the Company, acted as secretary of the meeting.[1] On motion duly made, seconded and unanimously carried, Mr. T. and Mr. U. were appointed scrutineers.[2]

Notice of meeting

Notice calling this meeting of shareholders was sent to all registered shareholders of the company on [*date*] in accordance with the bylaws [*or* articles] of the company, as evidenced by the declaration of Mr. . . . . , Clerk of the Stock Transfer Department of the Trust Company, Registrar and Transfer Agent of the Company. The declaration is annexed to these minutes as Schedule "A".

Attendance

The chairman requested that all the shareholders present give their names to the scrutineers and deposit all proxies with the scrutineers. [*If proxies are required to be deposited before the meeting (Rule 199) omit reference to them.*]

The scrutineers reported that there were shareholders present in person holding a total of . . . . shares, and that there were represented by proxy a total of . . . . shares making a grand total of . . . . shares represented in person and by proxy.

The chairman examined the proxies and declared that he was not adopting the scrutineers' report on attendance. The chairman declared that there were . . . . shareholders present in person holding . . . . shares and representing by proxy . . . . shares. The scrutineers' report on attendance is annexed to these minutes as Schedule "B".

---

[1] For variations, see Form 28A, *supra*.

[2] For variations, see Form 28B, *supra*.

Constitution of meeting

The chairman declared that notice of this meeting had been duly given to all registered shareholders of the Company in accordance with the bylaws of the Company, that there was a quorum present, and that the meeting was duly constituted for the transaction of business.

Minutes of last meeting

The chairman advised the meeting that the minutes of the last meeting of shareholders[3] were available for perusal by the shareholders and would be read if any shareholder so desired.[4] No shareholder made such a request, and on motion duly made by Mr. L., seconded by Mr. M., and unanimously carried, it was

RESOLVED that the minutes of the annual meeting of the shareholders held on the [*date*] be taken as read and verified.

Annual report

The chairman presented to the meeting the financial statement for the year ended [*date*] (including the balance sheet and accompanying statements, together with the auditor's report thereon) and the report of the board of directors, all contained in the annual report. The secretary read to the meeting the auditor's report for the year ended [*date*]. The following motion was made by Mr. G. and seconded by Mr. H.:

RESOLVED that the financial statement for the year ended [*date*] (including the balance sheet and accompanying statements, together with the auditor's report thereon) and all the transactions reflected thereby and the report of the board of directors, all contained in the annual report be approved.

Following the discussion a poll was demanded. A poll was taken and the scrutineers reported as follows: FOR . . . . AGAINST . . . .

The chairman examined the ballots and the scrutineers' report and declared that he was not adopting the scrutineers' report. The chairman declared the result of the poll as follows: FOR . . . . AGAINST . . . . and that the motion was carried [*or* defeated, *as the case may be*].

Election of directors

The chairman declared the meeting open for the election of directors and called for nominations. The following were nominated as directors: A, B, C, D, E, F and G.

On motion duly made, seconded and unanimously carried, nominations were closed.[5]

Since more than the required number of directors were nominated, the chairman directed that a poll be taken. The secretary distributed ballots and instructed the shareholders on the use of the ballots. The scrutineers collected the ballots and retired to complete the count. The meeting recessed for thirty minutes.

---

3 Unless required by the articles or the bylaws, reading or verifying the minutes of previous meetings is not necessary.

4 For variations, see Form 28E.

5 For variations, see Form 28F.

FORM 30—*continued*

The scrutineers reported to the chairman on the ballot for the election of directors as follows:

A . . . . shares
B . . . . shares
C . . . . shares
D . . . . shares
E . . . . shares
F . . . . shares
G . . . . shares

The chairman examined the ballots and the scrutineers' report and declared that he was not adopting the scrutineers' report. The chairman declared the result of the poll as follows:

A . . . . shares
B . . . . shares
C . . . . shares
D . . . . shares
E . . . . shares
F . . . . shares
G . . . . shares

and declared A, C, D, E and G duly elected directors of the Company to hold office until their successors are duly elected or appointed.

Appointment of auditor

The chairman declared the meeting open for the appointment of auditors.

The following resolution was duly moved by Mr. S, seconded by Mr. T:

RESOLVED that Messrs. Bee and Bee are appointed auditors of the Company to hold office until the next annual meeting or until their successors are duly appointed, and the board of directors be authorized to fix the remuneration of the auditors. [*Add if indicated:* on the basis of that presently paid.]

Conclusion

On motion duly made by Mr. M. seconded by Mr. N., and unanimously carried, the meeting was concluded.

. . . .
      (*Chairman*)   (*Secretary*)

VERIFIED at the meeting of shareholders held . . . .

. . . .
      (*Chairman*)

FORM 31

Minutes of Board Meeting (General Form)

MINUTES of a meeting of the board of directors of NAME COMPANY LIMITED, held at . . . . [*place*] on . . . . [*date*] at . . . . [*time*].
PRESENT . . . . being all [*or* a quorum] of the directors of the Company [and . . . . by invitation of the board].

Formalities

Mr. A, president of the Company, acted as chairman of the meeting, and Mr. B, secretary of the Company, acted as secretary of the meeting.[1]

Notice convening the meeting having been sent to all the directors in accordance with the bylaws [*or,* articles] of the company, and a quorum being present, the chairman declared the meeting duly constituted for the transaction of business.[2]

Minutes of last meeting

Minutes of the previous meeting of the board were read by the secretary and, on motion duly made, seconded and unanimously carried, it was

RESOLVED that the minutes of the previous meeting held on . . . . be verified.[3]

Business of the meeting

[*Set out the business conducted at the meeting, inserting Form* 31B *or* 31C *if applicable.*]

Conclusion

There being no further business, the meeting was concluded.

. . . .
        (*Chairman*)   (*Secretary*)

We, the undersigned, verify the above minutes and acknowledge having received [*or* waived] notice of the meeting. We approve all the resolutions passed and business transacted thereat.

. . . .
               . . . .

31A. Variations—Minutes Taken as Read

(i) *On Motion*

On motion duly made, seconded and unanimously carried, it was

RESOLVED that the minutes of the last meeting of the board held . . . . as mailed to every director be taken as read and verified.

(ii) *Without Motion*

Minutes of the last meeting of the board held on the . . . ., copies of which had been mailed to each director, were taken as read and were verified.

31B. Resolution to Call Annual Meeting

Calling of annual meeting

On motion duly made by Mr. M., seconded by Mr. N. and unanimously carried, it was RESOLVED:

(1) That an annual meeting of the shareholders of the Company be held as soon as convenient and that the secretary be authorized and directed to do all things necessary or desirable for the purpose of convening such a meeting;

---

[1] For variations, see Form 28A, *supra.*

[2] For variations, see Form 28B, *supra.*

[3] For variation, see Form 28E, *supra.*

FORM 31—*continued*

(2) That the draft form of annual report to the shareholders the notice of meeting and proxy form in favour of D., or him failing E., as presented to the meeting, be approved, the president having authority on the advice of the company's solicitor to make such changes therein as in his opinion are necessary or desirable;

(3) That proxies for use at the annual meeting of shareholders be deposited with the secretary of the Company not less than 48 hours (excluding Saturdays and holidays) before the time of holding of such meeting and that the shareholders be so notified.

31C. Resolution to Call General Meeting

Calling general meeting

On motion duly made, seconded and unanimously carried it was RESOLVED:

(1) That a general meeting of the shareholders of the Company be held as soon as convenient for the purpose of .... and that the secretary be authorized and directed to do all things necessary or desirable for the purpose of convening such a meeting;

(2) That the draft form of notice of meeting and proxy form in favour of D., or him failing, E., as presented to the meeting be approved, the president having authority on the advice of the Company's solicitor, to make such changes therein as in his opinion are necessary or desirable;

(3) That proxies for use at the general meeting of shareholders be deposited with the secretary of the Company not less than 48 hours (excluding Saturdays and holidays) before the time of holding of such meeting, and that the shareholders be so notified.

FORM 32

Minutes of Board Meeting Following Annual Meeting

MINUTES of a meeting of the board of NAME COMPANY LIMITED, held at .... on .... at ....

PRESENT .... being all [*or* a quorum] of the directors of the Company [and .... by invitation of the board].

Chairman and secretary

By resolution duly made, seconded and unanimously carried, Mr. A. acted as chairman of the meeting and Mr. B. as secretary of the meeting.

Constitution of meeting

The chairman declared that all [*or* a quorum] of the directors being present in person, (and having waived notice[1] of calling the meeting) the meeting was duly constituted for the transaction of business.

---

[1] In some jurisdictions the statute and often the articles or bylaws provide that no notice is required for routine business conducted by the board immediately after an annual meeting. In this case use: This being the first meeting of the board held immediately after the annual meeting, the chairman declared that there was a quorum present and that the meeting was duly constituted for the transaction of business.

Minutes of last meeting

The minutes of the previous meeting of the board were read by the secretary and, on motion duly made, seconded and unanimously carried, it was

RESOLVED that the minutes of the previous meeting of the board held
.... be verified.[2]

Election of officers

On motion duly made, seconded and unanimously carried, it was

RESOLVED that the following persons be elected or appointed officers of the Company, to hold the office referred to opposite their respective names for the ensuing year or until their successors are duly elected or appointed:

President:	A............
Vice-President:	B............
Secretary:	C............
Treasurer:	D............

Conclusion of meeting

There being no further business, the meeting was concluded

....
      (Chairman)   *(Secretary)*

We, the undersigned, verify the above minutes and acknowledge having waived notice of the meeting. We approve all the resolutions passed and business transacted thereat.

....
....
     ....

---

[2] For variation, see Form 28E.

TABLE OF CASES

Page

D

E

TOPICAL INDEX

References are to Rule Numbers in Part I unless otherwise stated.